Watching My Friend Die

The Honest Death of Bob Schwartz

Mark Hare

ACTA

ASSISTING CHRISTIANS TO ACT

PUBLICATIONS

Watching My Friend Die
The Honest Death of Bob Schwartz
by Mark Hare

Edited by Gregory F. Augustine Pierce
Cover design by Tom A. Wright
Cover art "Passing" by M.P. Wiggins, www.TheSpiritSource.com
Typesetting by Desktop Edit Shop, Inc.

Published by: ACTA Publications
                  Assisting Christians To Act
                  4848 N. Clark Street
                  Chicago, IL 60640
                  800-397-2282
                  www.actapublications.com

Library of Congress Catalog number: 2005920914
ISBN: 0-87946-284-1
Printed in the United States of America
Year 10 09 08 07 06 05
Printing 10 9 8 7 6 5 4 3 2 1

Contents

A Note from the Publisher

How does one write a book about the death of friends? If you try to generalize about the death of all friends (or even the deaths of all *your* friends), you run the risk of missing the uniqueness of each friend's life…and death.

Mark Hare has avoided that mistake in *Watching My Friend Die*. He has written about the death of all friends by writing about the "honest death" of one specific friend, Bob Schwartz, in great detail—not because he thinks you know his friend or even care about Bob Schwartz. Hare writes about the death of his friend to explore the very nature of death itself and the human instinct to fight it until the end.

He also writes about the death of his friend to explore the nature of life, using his own serendipitously renewed friendship with Bob Schwartz as the grist for his reflective mill.

Why should you read this story of Bob Schwartz's death and Mark Hare's struggle to understand and come to some sort of peace with that death? Because you, too, have had a friend die, or soon will, and you will need to understand and come to peace with *your* friend's death.

But you must also come to grips with your *own* death, for you are someone's friend, and you are going to die someday. What really matters is how you have lived your life and what kind of friend you have been to others.

This is a very Catholic book—not just because both Bob Schwartz and Mark Hare are cradle Catholics but because they both have a very Catholic way of looking at the world. Their view is incarnational, sacramental, relational, familial and hopeful. It is accepting of suffering and death yet grasping for life and resurrection with every breath. Thus it is a fitting contribution to *The American Catholic Experience* series of first-person reflections on what it means to be a lay Catholic in the last part of the twentieth and the first part of the twenty-first centuries.

So read *Watching My Friend Die* not for Bob Schwartz nor for his family nor for Mark Hare nor even for your own friends. Read this book for yourself, and then let your tears flow for the human condition.

Gregory F. Augustine Pierce
President and Co-Publisher
ACTA Publications
Chicago, Illinois

Introduction

Sometimes death comes like a bolt from the sky—a car accident, a plane crash, a burst aneurysm, an armed robbery.

More often, though, the character of our death is a product of the life we live, of the choices we have made over decades. I never quite thought about it that way until Bob Schwartz, a high school acquaintance I had not seen in thirty years, reached out to me in the last eighteen months of his life.

His dying taught me that our popular expectations of death are plain wrong. We expect people to go quietly when it's their time. We expect people to *know* when it's their time. Part of the myth of dying is that when we get old or very sick, we can simply *decide* to go, having made our peace and settled all our scores.

We romanticize the idea of dying at home, surrounded by loving family members. But we are aghast when dying people let themselves become a burden to family and friends. It is not OK to "impose," to ask loved ones to be patient, to take one's time checking out, to fight death even when it is inevitable. This idealization of the good death is so powerful that it colors what we see. As my friend was dying, I kept waiting for the "good" death to kick in. I expected that at some point Bob would turn on the autopilot and shut himself down on schedule.

But we don't control our departure any more than we control our entrance into this world. And the expectation of a good, quick, neat death is itself a burden on the dying person. We cannot control the *circumstances* of our death, but we can control the *character* of our death.

Bob Schwartz died the "wrong" way. He held on when there seemed to be no reason, when it appeared that he was just selfishly imposing his preferences on his family. But there was nothing selfish about Bob. He was not perfect, nor without ego, of course, but his whole life was spent sustaining and nurturing an expansive network of family and friends.

The expectation of the good death ignores the fact that in death we are the same person we are in life—a product of choices made and habits formed. Choosing good over the course of a lifetime is important. The circumstances of death are not.

Bob was the hub; his family and friends were the spokes. He took his strength, his hope, even his faith in God from the people in his life. His death, though long and difficult, was a reflection of his life. He died trying to connect to people because that is how he lived. He needed his friends to help him cross into the next life.

He was a teacher who kept track of former students and their parents. He was a musician who nudged his way into the local club scene in Rochester, his hometown. He nudged his way also into the lives of famous musicians he admired—John Denver, Tommy Makem and Steve Goodman. He learned their tricks and wrote songs about silly things and life-and-death things, and he wrote them all for his friends. It was part of his job—sustaining and nurturing community.

He wasn't much of an athlete, but he willed and worked himself into a job as assistant hockey coach at McQuaid Jesuit, the high school where he taught for twenty-five years. He did it because he liked being part of the team, being the historian who could tell the players exactly what to expect from the next opponent. He coached as he lived—never sweating the small stuff, just teaching respect and duty and the value of being part of something bigger than self.

He took the memories of people who had inspired him somehow

and turned them into parables that he would tell over and over to every new class. He used the stories to stay connected to people he loved and to connect young people to the ideals he always tried to live.

Bob didn't care what he wore. It didn't bother him that he was driving a twenty-five-year-old car (a car that was just an old wreck, not a cool antique). He loved teaching at McQuaid, and he didn't care that he was working for Catholic-school wages. He knew what it meant to be rich, and he knew it had nothing to do with money.

He was never too busy to talk. He was always the initiator—the guy who would call you up out of the blue and start right where you left off with him ten years earlier. He was never too busy to drop what he was doing to help a friend.

Bob was diagnosed with cancer of the pancreas in January 1997; he lived until November 1998—a period of twenty-two months. The final months were especially painful, but Bob did not surrender.

In those last few months, I offered to write his story, expecting to turn his life into one of those parables he was so fond of. I was deeply moved by his courage and by the love and loyalty of his family and friends. I have rarely known anyone who had such a profound impact on so many lives. But the story of Bob's death wasn't easy to understand, let alone easy to write. When I began this project, I thought it would be another *Tuesdays with Morrie*—in which Morrie Schwartz approaches his own death with peace and acceptance, discussing what he has learned along the way with his former student Mitch Albom.

But my friend wasn't like that at all. He never talked about death, except to joke about it. He did not offer soliloquies on the meaning of life as his final gift. He didn't find meaning in death. He found meaning in life, in holding on to it with all his strength.

He knew he was dying, but he tried to convince himself that he could have a normal life again if he would but stick with his routine and set goals to keep himself moving forward.

He knew he had touched many lives. But near the end, he worried that he had not done enough. His ego needed reassurance. He wanted to know that he would be remembered, that his legacy would not die with him.

Bob was a very good man. His poetry was insightful. He was incredibly good at remembering names and putting people at ease. His humor knew no limits. His struggle was compelling not because he was one-of-a-kind but precisely because in every way that matters Bob Schwartz was Everyman: He was afraid to die; he surely didn't want to die alone; he wanted to be sure he mattered, but he was insecure enough to doubt that he did.

> *His struggle was compelling not because he was one-of-a-kind but precisely because in every way that matters Bob Schwartz was Everyman.*

We Catholics have a phrase for the connection among all believers, living and dead. We call it the "Communion of Saints." We profess our belief in it every time we say the Apostles' Creed, yet we never reflect on what it means or why it matters. Most of us, including most Catholics, see our relationship to God as a private, one-on-One (if you will) affair. But the church teaches that we all approach God together—the living and the dead approach God together. Now *that* is a radical way of looking at things.

So we Catholics believe we can actually intercede for each other before God. We believe the saints who have gone before us can petition God for grace to help us live holier lives. We also believe we can help our "dearly departed" to transition from temporal life to eternal life. We are always aware of the continuum of life and the impact each individual soul has on the whole. Thus to believe in the Communion of Saints is to proclaim that no death is private.

Instinctively, we all want to distance ourselves from death. I wanted to run away from watching Bob die, but for some very deep and spiritual reason I did not. I hung out with him for those last months of his life, and in the process I finally began to understand that dying is part of life. It seems obvious to me now—but it didn't at the time—that human beings are supposed to learn about life from death.

The Catholic concept of the Communion of Saints is a good way to think about this. We cannot buy ourselves a single extra minute of life by hiding from death, by pushing it into a closet and pretending it will not come for us. But when we think of ourselves as part of a larger community (a "communion"), it is easier for us to approach the death of one of our friends or family because we know that death is not the end—neither of our loved one nor of our collective existence.

Bob lived for others and was not afraid to depend on others when he needed them at the end. There is nothing wrong with that. It is not a sign of weakness, but a sign of humanity. It is countercultural, however. In our secular lives we admire rugged individualism. We see both achievement and failure as personal, not corporate.

Bob died as he lived—drawing himself closer to God through his relationships. Anyone of any faith can appreciate his struggle. This book, however, is not the biography of a teacher/songwriter from Rochester, New York. It is a search for universal truth by observing the experience of one man at the end of his earthly life.

Through my friend Bob Schwartz, I learned that to choose life is to live it fully, right up to the very end. Bob chose well—and that is all that mattered to him. That was his story. It became my story. It can become your story too.

Mark Hare
Rochester, New York
January 2005

No Telling What You May Find

Mark? This is Bob Schwartz."

I recognized his voice, even though I hadn't heard it in thirty years. My pulse quickened; my thoughts raced; I started to speak, stopped, and started again—all within a fraction of second. I was nervous, searching for the right word, the right tone, a way to disguise the irrational rush of guilt I suddenly felt.

I knew Bob had cancer. I even knew he might be dying. I work as a columnist for the *Democrat and Chronicle* in Rochester, New York. There had been two stories in the paper about the assistant hockey coach at McQuaid Jesuit High School who had been diagnosed with cancer of the pancreas. With one story, I had seen a picture of the Schwartz family and friends celebrating Mass in their living room. I recognized Bob from the photo and knew he was the same Bob Schwartz I knew in high school seminary. It was a long time ago. But I remembered him.

I knew there had been fundraisers for Bob, to help the family with his out-of-pocket medical expenses. When I read the stories, I told myself that this was just a guy I barely knew in high school, not someone I had an obligation to help any more than I had a duty to help all the other cancer patients out there. I felt sorry for them, but what was I supposed to do? You know how it goes. I read the stories about Bob, but dismissed his predicament as "none of my business." I didn't want to barge in where I felt I was neither needed nor wanted.

In my heart, of course, I knew better. I should have at least dropped him a note, maybe enclosed a small check. But when someone I know is very sick and likely to die, I never know what to say: "How are you feeling?" or "What's new?" I feel awkward, so I procrastinate and eventually avoid the situation if at all possible.

In this case, it was certainly possible, at least until Bob called me. I had convinced myself he wouldn't remember me anyway, but really I was just afraid of thinking about death if I didn't have to.

Like most people my age, I've seen grandparents die, aunts and uncles, too, and even my father, but that was different. They were older; it was "their time" to go. But Bob was my age, and I didn't want to get too close to him. Quite frankly, I didn't want to be reminded that people in their forties get cancer and die.

But Bob, being Bob, found me. Now I had no place to hide. I took a breath and pretended I knew nothing at all was wrong.

"Bob Schwartz, I remember you. How are you?" There it was, the stupidest question you can ask a person you know is dying. What was he supposed to answer: "Oh, I'm fine, except for the dying part."

I was hiding in the tall grass, hoping to conceal my discomfort, but Bob didn't care. He didn't want to talk about his death either. He was just angry with his medical insurer and wanted me to help. He quickly told me of his cancer diagnosis, of his radiation and chemotherapy treatments. He said the treatments had been successful and that he was optimistic, but he had discovered what he thought was a promising experimental treatment for pancreatic cancer (which often kills within months of diagnosis), yet his insurance company wouldn't cover it.

To be evaluated as a candidate for the treatment at the Stehlin Institute in Houston, Bob needed a fresh CT-scan, which he'd already received, but his insurance company was balking at paying for it, insisting that Bob was not covered for experimental treatments.

He wanted to know if I'd write about his predicament in my column and rattle the corporate cages. He wasn't asking to be covered for the experimental program, just for the tests that would determine his eligibility. If he were deemed a good candidate, there would be no cost to participate.

Bob was direct, even pushy. He had no problem asking me for a huge favor, even though our paths hadn't crossed in decades. But I would discover soon that he never expected anything of anyone that he would not happily do himself if he could. Bob assumed that someone was a friend for life until he or she proved otherwise—and even then he was hard to shake. He took great pleasure in being there for others, and he assumed others would be just as happy to be there for him.

I was glad to write about Bob's situation. An insurance company denying benefits (even for legitimate reasons) to a dying cancer patient is what we call in the trade a "columnist's relief act." I went to see him the next day, and he greeted me on his front lawn. He was slightly tanned; his muscle tone was normal; he had a little paunch; he looked healthy and vital—not at all what I was expecting.

We went inside and I met his wife Patty for the very first time. She is a small woman, with a clear voice and a hearty laugh. Her sense of humor is as biting and sometimes as dark as Bob's. On our way to the pool deck, we stopped in a basement family room that was filled with plaques and pictures and awards—mementos of Bob's and Patty's years together and of Bob's career both as teacher and musician. (I knew Bob was a guitarist and songwriter and had played in Rochester nightclubs and honkytonks with his group the Penny Players since college, but never once had I gone to see him.)

There were two large Tupperware tubs filled with recent letters and postcards—more than 2,000 greetings in all. And most of them were not from current McQuaid students but from former students and the parents of former students. Many of these messages were long and detailed descriptions of lives that had been influenced by a single teacher decades earlier.

This was my first glimpse of Bob's world—an expansive network of people who felt connected to him and to each other through him. I learned later that people who had known Bob only briefly or casually never forgot him. And he never forgot a face or a name. People loved him because he made them feel good about themselves and because he was a portal. ("Need a contact in Boston, or the name of a lawyer you can trust, or the words to some obscure 1960s folk song? Call Bob Schwartz; he'll know.")

People loved him because he made them feel good about themselves and because he was a portal.

I had left the newsroom to drive to his home that afternoon still feeling guilty about having ignored an old acquaintance who was in trouble. By the time I returned to work, I was yet another friend of a remarkable man. I felt welcomed, appreciated, and glad there was something I could do for him. That was Bob's way.

The three of us sat around a table, sipping iced tea. It was a sweltering day, so Bob backed his chair into a small arc of shade. "The tumor is now what they call an 'imperceptible mass,'" he said. "If I didn't *know* I had cancer, I wouldn't believe it."

But Bob wanted to cover every base. Even though he felt fine and even though the chemo and radiation treatments he had received had gone well, he was interested in the Stehlin program. He'd been to Texas to visit the institute and find out if he'd qualify for treatment with the experimental drug. He had already written a letter to the insurance company asking for support, his words reflecting a man who was angry at the system and dead serious about fighting for his life.

He wrote that his application to Stehlin had been supported and encouraged by his oncologist and primary care doctor. While he had been told that he was not then a good match for the program (because his tumor had responded so well to the chemo and radiation), he planned to return periodically to Texas for reevaluations.

That first visit, he said in his letter to his insurer, amounted to his seeking a second opinion, "and second opinions are covered in my contract."

Then he wrote, "In my twenty-seven years of membership [in the health plan], I have had one claim for myself—an emergency room visit in Troy, New York.... I've never spent a night in the hospital in forty-nine years, never missed a day of work due to illness [until] I was leveled with the news in January, 'I'm sorry, Bob, but you have pancreatic cancer and only months to live.' Well, I intend to battle this disease with or without the help of my insurance carrier.... Please realize that it's a lot easier to fight this disease with people and companies saying, 'We're behind you, go for it, don't worry,' than with them saying, 'You can't do that,' or 'CLAIM DENIED.'"

In that letter was the key to Bob's plan—and to his essence: "It's a lot easier to fight this disease with people and companies saying, 'We're behind you....'" Bob did nothing alone. He would not fight cancer alone, nor would he face death alone. As we talked on the deck that day, I felt myself being drawn into his life. I identified immediately with his anger and frustration. He had been told that he could be dead in a few months. His doctor suggested an experimental program (no guarantees, of course, but cause for hope), and bureaucrats at an insurance company had turned him down without even talking with him. I imagined myself in his predicament: I'd be writing letters; I'd be screaming into the phone; I'd be outraged to think that some company would let me die to save a few bucks.

But I was interested in something more than the details of Bob's situation. As one of his fellow teachers later told me, Bob had a Gatsby-like quality. When you talked to him, you felt you were the only person in his world and you wanted to be his friend.

Bob was in full battle mode—angry, ready to fight, but hopeful and realistic at the same time. He was impressed by the work at Stehlin but unimpressed with all the quack cures he'd discovered on the Internet or people had suggested he try.

We talked a bit about Cardinal Joseph Bernardin, the archbishop of Chicago who had died from pancreatic cancer the year before. It was a horrible death, but Bernardin had gradually come to see death as a friend and he embraced it in the end. He had even written a best-selling book, *The Gift of Peace*, about his experience.

But Bob wasn't buying any of it. "Maybe when I'm in my seventies, I could do that," Bob said, "but I'm forty-nine. I can't even think about not fighting this or even of retiring from my job. It's funny. My attitude since I got married and had kids was to pray that nothing bad ever happens to them, but I forgot to tell God I didn't want anything bad to happen to me until I'm seventy-nine!"

Bob said he hoped to go back to work at McQuaid come September, but he had already agreed to take a job in the development office and leave the classroom, because he didn't want to die on the kids in the middle of the school year. "When I got cancer," he said, "I told the kids at school not to pray for me to get better and then get mad at God if I die. Prayer is not deal-making."

I found myself impressed. Bob had it just right. Before I left that afternoon to go back to the paper he half whispered to me, "I really can't find anything negative in this whole experience. It's even got people I know going back to church."

I knew we'd talk again. Soon.

The title of this chapter, "No Telling What You May Find," is a line from a song called *The Last Jump*. Bob wrote it in memory of his father, John Schwartz, a paratrooper in the Second World War. The song evokes the terror of a nighttime jump into enemy territory—a leap men can take only with the support of friends. "Into the black; no turning back; no telling what you may find."

That afternoon on Bob's deck, I began to shed a lot of my apprehension about getting too close to death—not because I was suddenly comfortable with death but because Bob didn't seem to be dying at all. I thought maybe he'd beat the cancer, that maybe he already had. For sure I thought he'd be a good story: Local teacher beats the odds.

I confess that if Bob had been flat on his back that day, with the pallor of death on his face, I might very well have never come back. But his optimism was refreshing and engaging; he seemed to have his emotions in balance. Here was a man who was indignant at being turned down for a CT-scan but careful not to encourage his students to shake their fists at God in anger if he died.

I left that day hoping—and at a certain level expecting—that Bob would cheat death and that his victory would make a nice little story, one that would make me feel a little less vulnerable to death myself. When I look back on it, however, what I was really drawn to in Bob was the way he kept making the right choices: going back to work, but changing jobs; seeking out new treatments; staying in touch with his friends; telling jokes and putting on a smile. None of these things could stop the cancer, but by making several positive choices every day, Bob kept control of his *life*. He did not make room for the cancer; he forced the cancer to make room for him.

Who Are You?

I learned during Bob Schwartz's eulogy that "Who are you?" was his signature question. He would challenge his students with it again and again as a way of making them think about who they were becoming. It was his way of helping young men realize that who they are is a matter of choice, not fate.

So who did Bob chose to become? What was it about him that made such a lasting impression on the people who crossed his path?

When I first started to write his/my story in my head, I kept focusing on the things that made Bob different. It took me years to finally understand it wasn't his eccentricities that were compelling but his humanity. He fought like hell to beat cancer because he loved life and feared death. *Who doesn't get that?* He wanted to be sure he had mattered. *Who doesn't get that?* He wanted to be loved. *Who doesn't get that?*

Bob was the kind of person who could bore into your soul, who could make you reexamine your own life through his trials. He gave witness to life, and he gave witness to death.

Part of the attraction was his intensity—not a raving, loud, jockish intensity but a quiet, centered interest in other people. His voice was soft and easy, a little raspy but never on edge. His eyes would find yours in a split second. Especially with students, he could sense pain or anxiety immediately. He could make it better with a little half smile or a simple greeting, or if necessary a serious reminder that 'Mom and

Dad really do care, no matter what it seemed like in their moment of anger.' Bob had a gift for empathy and a gift for finding the right word. He also had the memory of an elephant. He never forgot a word you said to him. He could pick up a conversation three years after it ended as if not a minute had intervened.

These are powerful assets. They helped to make him a natural teacher and a good friend and family man.

But they do not begin to explain who Bob was.

Music, especially folk music, was a big part of Bob's life. He played it. He wrote it. He used it to make a point or teach a lesson. It made him feel alive, and he wanted to share that feeling with others. But Bob was not content to listen to other people's songs and play them. Despite his shyness, he was determined to know the musicians he admired. Not, I think, because he wanted to learn how to play better, but because he wanted to understand their passion and make it his own.

His quest began early, in the summer after his high school graduation. On a trip to New York City, he stopped a young man carrying a guitar through a hotel lobby. Bob asked if he could see it, and thus made the acquaintance of John Denver, then playing with the Chad Mitchell Trio. A year later, on another New York trip, he looked up Denver, who was in town for a music festival. The two of them had dinner and some long conversations over the weekend, and that meeting grew into a lifelong, cross-continental friendship. Over the years, Bob also found ways to meet and learn from Harry Chapin, Steve Goodman and John Prine.

I'm sure Bob discovered the great Irish folksinger Tommy Makem, as I did, when he was performing with the Clancy Brothers on *The Ed Sullivan Show* and others in the 1960s. Makem, who grew up in County Armagh, Ireland, learned traditional Irish songs at his mother's knee and mastered the banjo and tin whistle. He made his way to New York City in the 1950s, chasing his dream of becoming a professional performer. In the early 1970s, Bob heard Tommy Makem play in concert in Rochester and decided that he'd find a way to meet up with his hero when he next appeared in town. How Bob got himself appointed to chauffeur Tommy around town is still a mystery to everyone.

His connections to professional musicians made Bob part of a community that extended well beyond Rochester and McQuaid.

But Tommy remembers landing at the Rochester airport a year later, being greeted by Bob Schwartz. "Then every time I came to Rochester, he was there. And I discovered that he had this great passion for folk songs. So the talk was always folk songs, and then too, about school, his teaching and coaching hockey."

"I have spent my whole life in this business," Tommy says, "but Bob would know things I wouldn't even have thought about—song titles, lyrics, authors. He was a man who was absolutely dedicated to anything he was doing. And whatever it was, he did it wholeheartedly."

Paul Lindsley, a college classmate of Bob's, tells about a weekend he and Bob spent at a songwriting workshop in Philadelphia run by Steve Goodman and John Prine. As the session was about to begin, Paul remembers Bob approaching from afar with John Prine. Somehow, Bob had located him and—perhaps over a few beers the night before—tried to learn anything he could about Prine's approach to music and life. "Bob could hook up with anybody," Paul says.

His connections to professional musicians made Bob part of a community that extended well beyond Rochester and McQuaid. He enjoyed the connection, and it was important to him—evidenced by the fact that he saved notes of his encounters and correspondence with musicians (all of which made my job easier when it came to writing this book).

To get himself into the Carnegie Deli with John Denver or to land himself a job as Tommy Makem's Rochester driver, however, Bob had to push beyond his comfort zone. He had to beat back his inclination to shyness and reach out—and the effort obviously made him a better person and teacher.

Teaching fit Bob's ideals like a glove. After graduation from St. John Fisher College in 1970, Bob got a job teaching fourth grade at St. Theodore's Catholic elementary school in suburban Rochester.

There he began to develop the teaching style that would endear him to so many. It was at St. Theodore's that he formulated the first of three stories—actually parables—that he would tell every student he ever taught.

Call the first parable, "The Lard Sandwich." There was a little boy in Bob's class who came to school with a lard sandwich for lunch. Bob was repulsed by it and came up with an idea—he'd pretend to draw a name out of a hat, with the lucky winner getting a McDonald's hamburger—provided by Bob—for lunch. Bob would make sure the lard-sandwich boy won. The other teachers discouraged him: "If you do it once, you'll have to do it every day." Bob heard their warning, but he didn't buy it. If he had to find a way to feed the boy every day, he would. And he did.

The moral of the story, according to Bob, is not to listen to people who tell you not to do the right thing because it's impractical.

The second parable is called "The One-Point Rule." As Bob told it, John Tette, a high school friend of his, flunked Latin by one point in his junior year of high school seminary. At the seminary in those days, Latin was a big deal. You had to pass it, but John just couldn't get it, so he had to transfer.

After high school, while Bob and most of the rest of us went off to college with student deferments, John didn't go to college. He was drafted and later killed in Vietnam—in August 1965, just fourteen months after he graduated from high school.

Bob told the story—sometimes as he took a class to Rochester's Vietnam Memorial and showed them John Tette's marker—and always said, "Kids, if you need one point to pass, I'll always give it to you. Grading is not an exact science."

The third parable, "The Neighbors," is the story of a family that once lived in the house next to the split-level ranch Bob and Patty owned. The parents went out to a holiday party between Christmas and New Year's, and the two teenage children went out with friends. When the parents returned, the father smoked a cigarette but didn't put it fully out. A little while later, with both parents in bed, a fire broke out in the kitchen. When the parents woke up, they each ran to one of the kids' bedrooms to awaken them and get them out to safety. It turns out that the kids hadn't returned home yet, but both mom and dad died of smoke inhalation on the bedroom floors. The moral of the story, Bob told innumerable high school kids who were having trouble with their parents, is always to remember that parents will lay down their lives for their children.

I don't know the accuracy of the Lard Sandwich parable. It's hard to imagine any parent sending their child to school like that. But the other two were certainly topped with dollops of rhetorical whipped cream.

John Tette may have flunked—or almost flunked—Latin. But his sister and brothers never heard it that way. "The way we remember it is that John just decided he didn't want to be a priest and so he left and went to Aquinas High School," says his sister, Therese. "When he graduated, I know one of my brothers tried to talk him into going to college, but he didn't want to; John was determined to join the Marines. He thought it was the right thing to do."

John Tette became an ammunition runner and was killed while carrying materiel to his squad. It was August 18, 1965. He was nineteen years old, the first Marine from the Rochester area to die in Vietnam, and the eighth of 280 local servicemen who lost their lives in that war.

But, Therese says, if The One-Point Rule story is not quite accurate, it is true to the spirit of their friendship. The Tette family, with ten children, and the Schwartz family, with seven, were friends and grew up together at Holy Family parish. Somehow over the years Bob had become convinced that a sympathetic teacher might have altered his friend's life path ever so slightly, and that doing so might have saved his life. That was the lesson he took to heart and shared with others.

As for The Neighbors, it's true that the children were out that night. But the parents probably didn't die trying to see if their children had yet returned home. The wife was found dead on the stairs, apparently having collapsed on her way to awaken her husband. Bob's version could be inaccurate on the details, but it was surely correct in principle. He may have embellished this and his other parables over the years, but the message was always clear: We take care of one another, no matter what.

The only other thing I know about Bob's three years at St. Theodore's is that he was somehow able to get Steve Goodman to come out one February afternoon in 1972 to play for the fourth and fifth grades. Bob kept notes from the occasion. After Goodman performed one night at a Rochester tavern, Bob approached him and told him that the fourth graders had been singing his song *City of New Orleans* and would really appreciate a sing-along with the songwriter. The next day Goodman obliged. Bob kept a listing of all the songs the kids sang with Goodman in the library of St. Theodore's: In addition to *City of New Orleans*, they did Tom Paxton's *I Left My Heart on a 747*, Kris Kristofferson's *Me and Bobby McGhee* (with Goodman yodeling at the end), the Beatles' *Here*

Comes the Sun, and Gene Autry's *Back in the Saddle Again.*

Bob Schwartz and Steve Goodman shared a common irreverence for mortality. Goodman battled cancer on and off for more than ten years before he died in 1984. A lifelong Cubs fan, Goodman wrote a song called *A Dying Cub Fan's Last Request* in 1981. If he hadn't written it, Bob would have. It is dripping with antipathy for the popular desire to shove the sick and dying off-stage:

> *So if you have your pencils and your scorecards ready,*
> *I'll read you my last request*
> *Give me a double-header funeral in Wrigley Field*
> *On some sunny weekend day (no lights)*
> *Have the organ play the National Anthem*
> *and then a little "na, na, na, hey hey, hey, Goodbye"*
> *Make six bullpen pitchers carry my coffin*
> *and six ground keepers clear my path*
>
> *Have the umpires bark me out at every base*
> *In all their holy wrath*
> *It's a beautiful day for a funeral, Hey Ernie let's play two!*
> *Somebody go get Jack Brickhouse to come back,*
> *and conduct just one more interview*
> *Have the Cubbies run right out into the middle of the field,*
> *Have Keith Moreland drop a routine fly*
> *Give everybody two bags of peanuts and a frosty malt*
> *And I'll be ready to die*

I Gave You Each Other

Because of who he was and how he lived, Bob Schwartz's cancer wasn't his alone. He would die from it, but others would learn from it.

Even before Bob was diagnosed in January 1997, Patty knew something wasn't quite right. During the Christmas break, he was uncharacteristically grumpy and angry. He thought he had a touch of the flu.

"He was not himself," she recalls. "He never said anything bad about me, or anything unkind. But there was a day right before he was diagnosed when he actually came looking for me. I was going to a hockey party for the mothers of kids on the team and he said, 'Why would you go? They don't like you anyway.' And that just continued. That kind of talk wasn't Bob. I knew something was wrong. But I was still angry."

Shortly after the Christmas break, one of Bob's fellow teachers noticed his jaundiced look. Bob didn't even want to check it out with the school nurse, but he finally relented. The nurse immediately ordered him to see his doctor.

As always, Bob and Patty tried to soften the anxiety with humor. Said she: "You're beyond yellow, Bob. If you fall down on a hardwood floor, I won't be able to find you." Of course, it was no joke, just her way of bracing for the biggest trial of their marriage.

Bob didn't visit a doctor any more than was necessary. He was like his father that way. He hated to be sick or even think about being sick. He preferred to deny all the little illnesses and will himself to feel better. But he liked Dr. Richard Gagnier, whose wife and nurse, Caroline, had been one of Bob's students at St. Theodore's. That link was reassuring to Bob. Connected to his friends, he felt stronger than he could ever be alone. He felt the bond of friendship would protect him.

Bob and Patty sat huddled together on a small chocolate-colored settee in Richard's cramped office. "He told me that he'd traveled some lately and eaten at a lot of different restaurants," Richard says. "He thought maybe he had hepatitis."

Patty didn't buy it because he had no symptoms other than jaundice. After some preliminary tests, Richard confirmed her diagnosis. "It's not hepatitis," he told them. Then he ordered an ultrasound of the abdomen.

"We talked about what it might be," Patty says. "Somebody told us that it might be diabetes, so we talked about using insulin and changing Bob's diet. We heard somewhere that if they found a spot, it might just be a gallstone. We didn't talk about cancer."

A few days later, Bob and Pat went to see the radiologist, actually *hoping* to see a spot on the ultrasound, and when one appeared they were giddy. "I remember jumping around and saying to Bob, 'Oh, it's just a gallstone,'" Patty says. "I told Bob, 'They can get rid of this. We're OK. Why'd I take a day off work for this?' The radiologist just stared at us. He was real quiet. He just said Dr. Gagnier would be waiting for us at one o'clock.

"It was only about eleven, so we had some time. It was a beautiful, crisp, sunny day and we drove around. We went to a drugstore. I was trying to quit smoking and needed some more patches. I went to the pharmacist and had a box of patches in one hand and cigarettes in the other. I told him about the spot they found with Bob's ultrasound and said, 'If you were me, which would you buy?' He said he didn't know what the spot was, but he added, 'I have to tell you the patches are better for you, but if I were you I'd take the cigarettes.'

"As we drove around, Bob was constantly touching me. He was short of breath, very tired and grumpy. We went right from the pharmacy to Dr. Gagnier's office. We couldn't go to lunch because we were just too nervous."

As Patty told me this story, I remembered all the ways I try to wish good news in my direction. I look for reasons to stay positive, to be happy. I do it even for little things. I surf the various weather forecasts and go with the one I like best. If one guy says we're going to get six to ten inches of snow and another calls for two to three, I trust the latter. When the spring training baseball magazines come out, I thumb through them to see which one says the best stuff about the Yankees. That's the one I buy.

When my dad was dying from emphysema in the spring of 1990, I would occasionally retreat in my mind and think about how we could celebrate his and my mom's fiftieth wedding anniversary—still three years away. It was as if I could buy us more time by planning for it.

When I started to write this book, I didn't shop it around to publishers to see if there was any interest, before I put the time in. I was pretty sure there would not be any interest, because nobody knows me and nobody knows Bob Schwartz. But I didn't want to invite discouraging words. I didn't want anyone to tell me not to bother because there is no market for a story like this. I needed to write this book, for Bob and for me. So I chose a rosy forecast. I expected success, even a best seller. All of this, I suppose, is a form of denial. But it is also a way to buy a little hope, to give myself a reason to hold on.

That's what Bob and Patty were doing that morning. That's what they would keep doing. They burnished every piece of bad news with hope—so they could slide over it and keep going.

When they arrived at Richard's office, there were no patients in the waiting room. Caroline saw the two of them and said, "Just one moment."

Bob and Pat could hear Richard and Caroline whispering, "Right away, I thought, 'Oh shit,'" Patty remembers. "Then Richard came out. He wasn't smiling. He looked like he was about to cry, like he just wanted to hug us. We went into his office and we sat down. He came around in front of his desk and leaned on it. He explained that what Bob had was not good, that it looked like a growth on the pancreas."

Bob wanted to believe the two of them could control the situation, that optimism could stop the cancer.

"A mass on the head of the pancreas, producing jaundice, is presumed to be cancer until it's proven to be something else," Richard told me later. Patty and Bob froze when Richard promised to "do everything we can to prolong your life." At that, she says, "We were numb. He could have been singing the *Star Spangled Banner*. After we heard 'we'll-do-all-we-can,' we didn't hear anything else."

Still, Bob wanted to believe the two of them could control the situation, that optimism could stop the cancer. Bob's instinct was to do what he had trained himself to do by decades of choices—reach out to others and take good news anywhere he could find it.

They had eight days to wait before a biopsy could be done, and they both knew that whatever was wrong was *very* wrong. "As soon as we knew this was serious, Bob's moodiness went away," Patty says. "He lay in bed wondering, 'What am I going to do?' He was clinging to me. He didn't want me out of his sight. He was so scared."

Dr. Vincent Chang, the surgeon who was to do Bob's biopsy, suspected cancer and was prepared to remove the tumor if possible. It was not possible; the cancer had spread too far, so Chang rerouted the intestine so it could drain and help with digestion. This took care of the jaundice.

Bob prepared for the surgery by asking Vicki Bida to be present in the operating room. Bob didn't know Vicki well, but her son Morgan had been in his class, and her daughter Katie was a good friend of Jenny Schwartz—Bob and Pat's daughter.

Vicki was training to be a physician's assistant at the time, so she asked Dr. Chang if it would be all right. He agreed that she could be present. "I think he thought that if I were in that operating room with him he would live through it," Vicki says.

Patty stayed with Bob in the hospital the night before the biopsy. He made her promise not to tell anyone how frightened he was. He wanted the people around him to mirror the optimism that the *public* Bob displayed—and feed it back to him.

Once Chang opened Bob, "he called me over," Vicki says. "'Feel this—feel the tumors.' So I reached into his belly. He said, 'Don't squeeze. I don't want to give him pancreatitis.' So I had his pancreas in my hands. I was honored, but I was embarrassed. He was not really a close friend."

The diagnosis was tentative, but accurate: cancer of the pancreas. "It was uncomfortable," Vicki says. "Right then, I wished Dr. Chang had said, 'No, it would be inappropriate for you to be in the surgery.' But he didn't, and that forced me to come into a chapter in Bob's life that I did not feel I was close enough to him to be in."

That's how Bob's dying would be. He would invite people, even those not close to him, to get close. It was uncomfortable at times. We all have privacy zones. It is difficult to sit through chemo with a friend or to spend the night in his room to make sure he doesn't wander under the influence of powerful painkillers. But Bob expected people to do that—just as he would have done for them.

It was not just his cancer; it was *our* cancer. We had to fight it together—to help him get better and to help ourselves confront our own mortality.

Meanwhile, as the surgery dragged on into hour five, the family's mood actually picked up in the waiting room. "We had been told, that if it goes over four hours, they're probably removing the tumor and he'd be all right," Patty remembers. "So once it went past four hours, we started telling jokes and skipping around the room."

When it was done, Vicki started down the stairs toward the family. She could hear them laughing and joking and realized Dr. Chang had not reached them yet. She turned and went back upstairs. Professionally and personally it would have been wrong for her to deliver the news. She was uncomfortable knowing what she knew before the family knew it. She had to take a step back.

Soon, Dr. Chang delivered the bad news to Patty. "He took my hand," she recalls. "He said he couldn't do much, that he had rerouted Bob's organs, but I wasn't listening very carefully." He said the cancer had progressed and that Bob probably didn't have much time, perhaps only several weeks to a few months.

"I was angry and had this knot in my stomach. I just hurt. I remember thinking, 'Take as many pictures as you can, right now, and sit and talk with him as much as you can.'" The memories began to flood back.

Bob Schwartz had met Patty Trinkaus in the summer of 1973 at the Red Creek, a popular nightclub. Patty had come to Rochester from Utica, New York, looking for work. They hit it off immediately and were married in November of that same year.

That summer, Bob was organizing a concert at Nazareth College to benefit research on Huntington's Disease, which had killed the legendary songwriter Woody Guthrie. Bob had somehow become acquainted with Woody's widow, Marjorie, and he invited her to speak about the disease at the University of Rochester and to attend the concert later the same weekend.

Patty loved being swept into Bob's circle of musicians and teachers. It was exciting; it was always interesting. And when Bob got cancer, she knew there'd be people around all the time. That was how they lived. She also knew she would have to fight his cancer with every bit as much determination as Bob.

A few days after they were married, a letter from John Denver arrived from Aspen. "Dear Bob, Annie and I both send our love and best wishes to you and Pat. Our wish for you is that your love grows with each passing day, that there are no Jet Planes in your life, and that your children know the beauty of flowers. I am very much looking forward to meeting Pat. Peace, John." It was a new life for Patty, and she embraced it.

After the surgery, while Bob was sleeping, Patty took a break and went home. Their son Eric, then a McQuaid sophomore, went home too. He crashed on his bed and pulled the pillow over his head.

As soon as his dad had been checked out for jaundice, Eric began searching the Internet. He did not shop around for more optimistic diagnoses to give himself a little more hope. It was a trick he had not yet learned. "The computer said it could be a sign of cancer," he remembers. "I hoped like hell it wasn't, but I had a real bad feeling. To tell you the truth, I wasn't really trying to figure anything out on my own. I was just real scared. For the most part I just didn't want to think about it. I tried to push it out of my head, especially when I was at McQuaid. When the tests came back that Dad didn't have hepatitis, I was more nervous. It's one of those things where you say to yourself: 'God, or whoever is in charge, isn't going to lay this one on me, is he?'"

His sister Jenny, then twelve, was also scared. "When they thought Daddy had hepatitis, I didn't know what that meant. I went into his room and he kept saying, 'I'm fine, I'm fine.' And I said, 'Dad, you're yellow.' But then when they said it was cancer and that he might die before my birthday, I was screaming. It wasn't fair."

After that, she was determined not to fall to pieces. "I never cried in front of Dad. Not once. I didn't want him to see me sad." That was her gift to Bob, and he was grateful for his little girl's spirit. His door was open throughout his personal war on cancer, and the only people he didn't want around were those who came to cry and say good-bye.

Patty wanted to be there when Bob awoke, so she returned to Genesee Hospital early that Saturday evening, thinking she might have to share the news she wished she could just erase. Bob was supposed to sleep through the night, but by the time she arrived, he was already awake and his room was full of people. They were all laughing and making jokes, and Bob was as usual the master of ceremonies.

There were so many people around that Patty couldn't get a word with him. He wanted to know the results of the biopsy, but she would not break the news in front of a crowd. That would have to wait until the next morning.

"I kept thinking, 'My God, in three months, I'm not going to have a husband. What am I going to do? All our plans are gone,'" Patty says.

Deep down, she never thought Bob could beat the disease. "The look on Dr. Chang's face said it all," she says now. But she resolved to fight it nevertheless. (That's what husbands and wives do for each other. You *have* to convince yourself to believe anything is possible. You choose the rosier forecast. It *could* be right, after all.)

Bob spent another week at Genesee, and the phalanx of visitors rarely slowed. It was almost a celebrity stay. The president of the hospital came down to see him. Bob had free TV and a phone. There were flowers and cards filling every inch of table and window ledge space.

Cancer was a community project for Bob. He could not have approached it differently. Many people, especially those who have outlived most of their families and friends, want to be left alone—except, perhaps, for a spouse or close friend. A former reporter at my paper died alone in her home and wasn't discovered for weeks. She had no close friends, no family anywhere near her. She was eccentric and kept people at a distance. When she left her job, she just went home and slowly disappeared.

She died as she lived: alone. She couldn't have done it any other way, just as Bob couldn't have pulled back to an inner circle of friends and family without feeling that he had surrendered. The crowds were as inevitable and necessary to him as the solitude was to that woman.

Bob's cancer was devastating for his friends. "Bob was the last person this should have happened to," his friend Paul Lindsley says. "I just kept thinking, this is a guy who spends his life doing things for people. This just wasn't right.

"He struggled all his life—with his own inadequacies, with his appearance, with all kinds of issues in his life. But he could always snap you back. After the surgery, it wasn't there. He couldn't rebound. I sat in the hospital with him. We were silent. When I left, all I could think to do was to kiss him on the forehead and say, 'I love you.'

"All those years, he was the historian, he was the convenor, now he was the focus." But it didn't last long. "As soon as he could get up, there he was, right back in his role."

Within a few weeks, Bob would write the song that summarized his hope and his expectation. It's called *I Gave You Each Other*. Here's the chorus:

> *Take care of each other*
> *You are all you've had*
> *In good times and in bad*
> *Be friends to each other*

In those few days in the hospital, Bob was already starting to look for signs that he would be all right—indicators he could use to will himself a victory over an enemy that was trying to bring him down. He would stay positive.

"If the nurse didn't bring him something to drink or some ice right on schedule," Patty says, "he'd say not to worry, they'll get it. His thing was, 'If they're not on top of me, I must be getting better.' If we'd go to the doctor's office and have to wait, Bob liked it. He'd say, 'I'm not an emergency. It's OK.' He liked not being an emergency."

He preferred a rosy forecast. He tried to make it real. In my time with Bob, I was seeing more clearly than ever that hope doesn't just fall into your lap. You have to choose it and live accordingly. By sharing his cancer with his friends, he did not bring people down. Rather, he gave them hope—and the tools to find it in themselves.

Suffer the Little Children

Back after I had just finished college, I took a job teaching religion at a Catholic girls high school in Rochester. I did it for six years, but I was no good at it, because unlike Bob I didn't have the knack for helping teenagers see the best in themselves and want to be better people because of it.

My approach was mechanical. I would assemble lesson plans and see them through, even when it was obvious the girls weren't getting anything from them. I would fill the time with worksheets and films and activities and speakers. But I couldn't connect any of it.

For several of those years I taught a course on marriage and sexuality, before I had a mature understanding of either. We did not promote birth control, obviously, but we did talk about contraception and how it works. I will never forget the student who approached me privately to say that she and her boyfriend were sexually active but—thanks to me—she understood how to prevent a pregnancy. "Whenever I think I'll need it," she explained, "I borrow a pill from my sister's pack."

Not only had I failed to persuade her not to become sexually active, I had left her ignorant of how the pill works—not to mention the problems I might have caused for her sister!

There were good days, to be sure, but mostly my frustration with teaching taught me to respect good teachers. I learned how difficult the job really is. One reason I turned to writing is because, at the end of the day, there is a product—a column or a story or a book. It is, of course, not that simple. It's nice to produce something, but a pile of papers filled with ineffectual writing isn't much of a legacy. I want the writing to make a difference, to change people's understanding and behavior. That is hard to judge or see, so as usual I pick the brighter forecast: I assume that my words of wisdom have hit home—even when I cannot tell for sure.

In teaching, however, you never see the product. You may see students change or improve over the course of a year, but you can't see what matters most—the adults those children become. Good teachers help students learn to make good choices—the right choices, the ones that will enable them to become adults of good character.

Like all good teachers, Bob Schwartz learned to be content with small rewards. He joined the faculty of McQuaid Jesuit High School in the fall of 1974. It was the perfect job for him. McQuaid was a community—a big extended family that embraced Bob and encouraged him to do what he did best. Just like a family would do.

He was hired to teach social studies, but his job was to help impressionable and confused young men become a part of something larger than themselves. His job was to teach them the values and discipline they would need to be good *men*. He didn't just talk about those values; he lived them.

He immersed himself in the McQuaid experience. He liked sports, though he was not much of an athlete. He would hang around the football players, the baseball players, and especially the hockey players. He skated a little as a young man, enough to learn to love that game, but the thing about Bob was that he didn't favor one group of kids over another. He was there as well for the "geeks," the loners, the kids who didn't know what they wanted to do. His classroom was open after school every day. Anybody who wanted to sit and talk or just do homework was welcome.

Bob started a string band as a way to engage another whole group of kids. Bob didn't just *do things;* he was *really present* for the kids. He paid attention to them, knew what they needed, and knew how to engage them.

Father Leon Hogenkamp, who was then the principal of McQuaid, remembers sitting in on one of Bob's classes that first year. There were twenty-eight boys in the class, and twenty-six of them participated in the discussion that day. That's pretty much unheard of in high school, but it was typical for one of Bob's classes. "He respected everyone," Father Hogenkamp says, "and the kids knew it and knew they had the freedom to speak and to be wrong."

Bob was not a scholar; he was a teacher who taught the lessons of a life lived well.

Paul Swiatek, class of '78 and a player in Bob's string band, found him pretty dry as a teacher, not at all charismatic—and yet Bob was the most influential teacher he ever had: "Bob's sacred way was this, 'Be yourself, and don't let what others think slow you down.' Of course, he never actually said that, but he said it with his actions."

The string band was a chance for kids to hang around with Bob for a couple of hours a couple of times a week. As much as Bob loved music, he was nothing close to a perfectionist. As with everything he did, Bob played music for the friendships, for the opportunity to connect. He didn't baby his guitar or worry about preserving the finest quality sound. He'd leave it out in the trunk of his beat-up Cougar ("Xavier Cougar," he called it) in the freezing cold. He owned a Guild D-40, with "a golden yellow spruce top—aged—like a piece of cheese in the fridge," Paul Swiatek says. The finish was crusted and cracked from being frozen. The top was warped near the bridge. At one point, after a Palm Sunday service, a loop of palms was woven into the turning pegs near the headstock, and there they rest to this day.

"That Bob didn't have a sense of how to care for his instrument mystified—and delighted—me," Paul marvels. He just let it "develop a bit of character." Bob treated his guitar like he treated his students—he loved them but didn't try to polish them up for show. He let them be what or who they were.

He could see in the students what they could not see in themselves.

To Paul, Bob was kind of a "mystic" who never really practiced or tried to get better at the guitar. He just played and enjoyed it. "And that was enough for him."

In a McQuaid alumni publication years later, Paul wrote a blurb about Bob: "I saw him get mad only once. Some kid in his class threatened another student, and they talked about fighting it out later on. Bob was furious. There was something in the stupidity of violence that grated against the very core of him."

He could see in the students what they could not see in themselves. Sometimes it would take years, and the advantage of twenty/twenty hindsight, for a student to finally hear what Bob had been saying. Paul Swiatek remembers that Bob once commissioned him to draw a portrait of his sister. Bob was convinced of Paul's artistic ability, even when Paul was not. "That is such a typical Bob Schwartz thing to do. He believed that I was good enough, even when I didn't—even when I really wasn't. I've always wondered what turns my life would have taken had I believed in myself as an artist and pursued it in college. If Bob had my artistic talent, I am certain he would have books filled with his drawings—doing it because it was part of him."

He taught kids to look beyond the obvious. Vicki Bida, the physician's assistant who helped during his biopsy, remembers a day when her daughter came home with a picture of the room where the Founders were discussing the Declaration of Independence. She was supposed to find eight things wrong with it. She found seven, but couldn't find that last one. Her brother Morgan, Bob's student, took one look at it and said, "The window's open. That's the other wrong thing."

How did Morgan figure it out? He remembered Bob saying in class that the Founders didn't want anyone to know what was in their hearts, that they were talking revolution. So they wouldn't have had the window open—even though it was sweltering.

Children were Bob's life. He was a Camelot idealist who believed the future would be as bright as the children who inherit it. While he was at St. Theodore's, Bob took offense at what he considered petty faculty squabbles. For him, all such tiffs were silly. The kids were all that mattered. That same school year, he wrote the song *Suffer the Little Children*, wishing that adults could learn as much from the little ones as the children learn from adults:

> *Suffer the little children to come unto me*
> *Become like the little children and someday you will see*
> *All of the treasures and all of the pleasures*
> *Of my holy kingdom to be*
> *And suffer the little children to come unto me*

> *Look how the little children, how they love one and all*
> *See how the little children come running when you call*
> *And if one takes a tumble, another might stumble*
> *But they laugh until everyone falls*
> *And look how the little children, how they love one and all*

> *Little children,*
> *All our wisdom is not in what we do*
> *In our haste to teach you love we fail to see*
> *How it lives to be*
> *In you*

Nourish the little children, for they are our seed
Cherish the little children in word and thought and deed
See the reflection of our imperfection
In loving direction they need
And nourish the little children, for they are our seed
And suffer the little children to come unto me.

"In our haste to teach you love, we fail to see how it lives to be in you." Indeed. That's what I mean about Bob's *being present*. As a teacher, I had to script everything. I was uncomfortable just listening. I didn't hang around after school to wait for a conversation that might give me some insight into the students I was teaching. Bob's gift was patience. He waited out the opportunity to make a point. He was open to the possibility of learning from the boys at McQuaid.

He chose to invest his life in children. He saw that as the best way to make a difference. He and Patty weren't able to have children of their own, so they adopted Eric in 1980 and Jenny four years later.

Bob was a doting father. He enjoyed waiting on the kids, helping them, listening to them, and watching them discover the world. He never pushed them to follow him into music or hockey or teaching.

Bob was never big on parish life, but he and Patty made sure their children were well churched—often inviting Jesuits from McQuaid to say Mass in their home with family and friends.

For themselves and the kids, Bob and Patty both wanted their home to be open, full of life and friends and family. While family was the center of his little community, the community was always expanding. And there was always room in the Schwartz home.

It was no coincidence that Bob and Patty's first home on Mayfield Street had an aboveground pool. His brother John says it was a good way to make sure there was always company. A lot of people don't want a pool for the same reason; they don't want their home to be a magnet for neighborhood kids or friends looking to cool off on hot summer days, but Bob and Patty welcomed it. Their second home, in suburban Penfield, had a built-in pool. It was an even bigger draw and helped make the Schwartz home a mini-Grand Central Station. That was by design, even though Bob couldn't swim.

Bob's love for his kids was simple and unconditional. There was no such thing as too much to ask. Jenny would call from a friend's house and ask for a Barbie toy or a scrunchie for her hair and Bob would drop whatever he was doing and drive it over. Sometimes he'd pack up and take Jenny to New York City to visit his sister Mary and do a little shopping and sightseeing—just the two of them. He went to all the soccer, baseball and football games. He didn't believe there is such a thing as "enough"—as in, "no more, I'm done, try me tomorrow."

I think that's why so many people tell me that Bob was simply the best person they ever knew.

Long Time Comin'

It's been a long time comin' and a long time gone
Been a few times right, been a few times wrong;
I've been in from the rain and been out in the cold;
One day I'm young and the next day I'm old

Thought I knew very well what I wanted to be
But my life started changing and the joke was on me

—Bob Schwartz

L ike many people, I used to think the best death is a quick death. No fuss. No muss. And please, no suffering. If I have to die, let it be in my sleep, or in a freaky accident so that I never know what hit me.

I don't think that way any more. We all fear death, but we fear dying even more. We dread the *process*. The slow deterioration, the loss of senses, the pain, the loss of control, the pity of family and friends, the return to a state of total dependence on others.

For a person who has lived well and hard and fully, who has called the shots for seventy-plus years, being diapered may feel like the ultimate indignity. But it is not. Dignity is not a function of physical vitality. Dignity is a product of choices made—of simple acts of love, forgiveness, tolerance; of consciously choosing hope when despair whispers in your ear; of trusting divine love when you are tempted to blame God for your predicament.

Dignity is acquired as people choose to respect life—their own and that of others. We don't lose our dignity when our teeth fall out, or when we start forgetting things, or when we lose control over our bodily functions. We lose our dignity only when we forget that we are part of the human family and act as if we are accountable to no one. We lose our dignity when we lose our humanity.

That is a hard lesson to learn in the abstract. When Bob Schwartz was diagnosed with cancer, he was a young man who was suddenly old—as his lyrics say. Life was changing and there seemed to be nothing he could do about it. The joke, as he sang, was on him.

After his biopsy, Bob alternated between bouts of deep sadness, even depression, and a public affirmation of life. He displayed a will, a commitment to get things done—because, as he came to believe, setting goals helped him stifle the cancer, at least in his mind.

He'd still crawl into bed and cry, afraid that he might die in a month. "No way, Schwartz," Patty would say. "I'll have to kill you first. We've got two teenagers and you're not leaving me all alone."

It was just the kind of reality check Bob needed to bring himself back from the edge and get focused on saving his life. He couldn't go back to teaching, but within a few weeks he was able to get himself back into the office to offer a little support to the McQuaid hockey team he helped coach, a team that was skating toward a city championship.

Bob was trying to do two things—stay alive as long as possible and convince himself that he had made a difference to the people in his life. His strategy was simple: stick close to his normal routine and allow his actions to tell his mind (and his cancer) that he would be OK.

Bob had reasons to live and was determined to give himself as many chances as possible. He knew the best way to stay alive was to get up every morning with a purpose and try to make a difference. Bob didn't so much worry about when he'd die. Instead, he concerned himself with making the biggest impact he could before the last day came. He showed no inclination to think back on his life or take stock of it.

The first of his many counterattacks on the cancer was a three-part TV news report done by Bill Pucko, sports director for R-News, the Rochester cable news outlet and a neighbor of the Schwartz's.

I still watch that video from time to time, just so I remember the sound of Bob's voice, his facial gestures, and how he moved. The first report begins with Bob skating during a hockey practice, wearing his black McQuaid hockey jacket and cap.

As he swooshes off the ice and sidles up to the camera, he says, "When I have this to look forward to, I don't have cancer. I'm going to church in about fifteen minutes, and I won't have cancer there either. I'll have prayers and people all around me. About the only time I have cancer is when I'm in the hospital."

The players, wearing Bob's initials "RS" on their helmets, were glad he was back on ice. Head coach Al Vyvenberg says the boys knew he was in a "life-and-death struggle, but they're handling it. They're pretty smart."

In the lead-in to his second report, Bill Pucko says: "His doctor calls him a perfect example of how to live with inoperable cancer. Coach Bob Schwartz is feeding off his vast support system that includes his family, the local music community, McQuaid hockey, and his Genesee Hospital medical team."

That's exactly what Bob was doing, and he says so in the next scene. As he takes a chemo treatment, Bob looks at the camera and says, "My doctors say if you can draw on the resources around you, it's going to make you better."

It was a message to his friends and to the people who were seeing him on TV for the first time: Don't give up. Don't you *dare* give up.

Looking back on it, Patty says they both knew even before the diagnosis was final that their lives would never be the same. "My job was to take care of Bob, that was it, nothing else." And he was "thinking about what to do next, what kind of impact he could make. It started on the table of the ultrasound and ended the day he died."

On the news clip, the reporter says the coach will be busy the next day when McQuaid plays for the Section Five championship in hockey and Bob plays at a fundraiser for himself at Milestones, a downtown Rochester nightclub.

As the chemo drips into his vein, Bob cracks a little joke: "Patty, tell me about our bills again." Then he settles into the lounge chair and looks again at the camera: "I have little patience for somebody who says, 'My day's ruined; I had a little rattle in the front of my car.' I tell you what, I'll trade you your rattle for some of the things that rattle my day."

As the segment ends, Bob is on stage at Milestones, introducing the song he wrote during chemo—*I Gave You Each Other*. It's the perfect anthem for the life Bob constructed and maintained up to the very end. Before he plays it on the R-News segment, Bob says playfully, "This is another song I wrote when I was writing under the name of God." Then he talks for a minute about a letter he received from a woman he did not know. It said, "I got pancreatic cancer seven years ago and they gave me six months to live."

In the final of the three reports, Bob and Patty are seated in their living room. "Our life as we knew it is gone," she says. "This is a new beginning." She talks about trips they'll take and how they are looking forward to the spring and going to ball games. Bob says, "It's like going into the big game thinking, we're gonna lose this, we're gonna lose this—then you'll lose. What bigger game is there than this?"

Bill Pucko concluded the report observing that since cancer had taken away his classroom, Bob hoped "he might still be able to teach…through TV."

The R-News reports elicited hundreds of cards and letters from well-wishers and energized Bob and Patty. Bob saw clearly that he could still have an impact, that his wrestling with cancer could inspire others to do the same, that it could give people hope. Thereafter, he seized every opportunity that came his way.

There were fits and starts. He began a journal, writing his thoughts in clean, clear strokes, never making a mistake—but reflecting very little on his personal battle with death. His journal was basically a hug-fest—Bob's way of saying what he thought people would like to hear after he was gone.

A fond memory was the last thing Bob hoped to become for people.

Still, there are a few touching entries, like the one dated April 2, 1997. Bob wrote that he isn't taking as much "heart" as Patty has from Dr. Chang's report that the tumor has become much "less pronounced." That was the day he also attended a wake for Brannon Smith, a McQuaid student who died of cancer. "I think I'll always remember Brannon as a fighter who tried everything to stay alive and fight the cancer. Sound familiar? Maybe someday someone will be writing that about me."

Of course, a fond memory was the last thing Bob hoped to become for people. His final entry came on July 20, when he wrote about my column on his dispute with his insurance company. "This will get the word out about my condition," he said, "and encourage others not to take the [insurance company's] first decision." Bob wrote that he'd start his new job as McQuaid's Director of Annual Giving the next day, and he promised to write more regularly. He concludes with a caveat: "No news is good news, tho." And there was no more news in the journal.

The fact is, I'm sure Bob found journal writing most unsatisfying. To merely record events, as he did, seems like such a waste of time when there isn't much time to be had. And yet, a searing reflection on the possibility of death would have focused his energy away from what really mattered to him—beating the enemy within. He had heard the odds; he knew most people lose to pancreatic cancer. But he made a point of refusing to be a statistic. He couldn't think about the next life, or wonder if there is a next life, without seeming to surrender to the inevitable loss of this life. Bob's approach was to will himself onward, to stay positive. So he put the journal aside and moved on to other strategies.

One of those strategies was to plan as if he had plenty of time. Almost as soon as he got out of the hospital, he went to the grocery store and bought a box of 500 coffeemaker filters, as a way to tell the disease that he wasn't about to die until he'd made 500 more pots of coffee, one pot a day. (And he was to get every one of those days—and 100 or so more.)

When Bob went to radiation or chemo treatment, he'd see other patients who had literally given up at the first mention of cancer, who had begun immediately to think of themselves in the past tense. Sometimes the doctors would ask him to sit for a while with someone who was like that. Sometimes it would help; sometimes it would not.

"I can't understand why people give up so easily," he'd say. "It's like they take this news as the gospel. The doctor might tell you you've got three months, but doctors don't know you. *Only you know you.* When they told me I had six months, I decided I'd beat it. And when I made it to six months, I'd decided to go for six more."

Dr. George Garrow, Bob's oncologist, learned the value of getting patients to help other patients from his sister. George grew up near

Pittsburgh, and his dream was to specialize in orthopedic medicine and one day become the Steelers' team doctor. "But while I was in med school, my sister got cancer, and as I spent time with her, I became aware that there was a big need for oncologists," he explains. His sister's cancer and death taught George to see death as part of life and its approach as a moment when people grow in new and marvelous ways. He never found oncology depressing. Patients always uplifted him.

When George's sister was diagnosed, she got a lot of help from others who had been through treatment; and later, she was the one doing the helping. George made this patient-to-patient buddy system a hallmark of his own practice.

Bob was a good buddy. "He never looked at the clock to see if his time was running out," George says. "Every time he'd come in, he helped me appreciate each day I have. We treated him fairly aggressively. He was otherwise healthy, his age wasn't a factor, and he had good support at home."

One of the patients Bob hooked up with—through a friend of a friend—was Tom O'Neill, a corporate auditor for Eastman Kodak, who took a company buyout offer in 1991. He then took up real estate sales. Tom and Carol O'Neill were married for forty-one years, never had any children, and probably would never have wandered into the Schwartz's circle were it not for Tom's pancreatic cancer.

But Tom and Bob shared both optimism and faith. From that, they forged a bond of friendship. "They had a strong phone friendship for a year," Carol says. "They would talk for hours. It was like a seesaw. If Bob was down, Tom was up and that was good for Bob—and vice versa."

After Tom was diagnosed, he started going to daily Mass. He made a point of visiting Carol's aunt in a nursing home, doing all he could to cling to normalcy and routine. He was making the choices that would both draw him closer to God and prepare Carol for his death.

Tom began making provisions for his wife. "He installed a new garage door," Carol says. "And bought and hooked up a new washer and dryer. He was making repairs—and he was doing it for me, to make it easier for me. He went to all of our friends—unbeknownst to me—and said, 'Take care of Carol for me.' He wanted me to go with him to H&R Block to do our taxes so I could meet the woman who handled our account. He was preparing me for life without him, and at the time I didn't see it."

Bob was paying attention, however, and eventually he would try to prepare Patty and the kids for life without him. Without even knowing it, Tom and Bob became not just friends but fellow paratroopers—there to make the last jump possible, there to help each other say yes when they wanted to say no. They had no idea how to die or how to get the most out of whatever time they had. But they helped each other to do what neither could have done alone.

In his first months with cancer, Bob stayed faithful to the normal rhythms of his life as a way to deny the disease a beachhead in his consciousness. He was not comfortable as the patient. But now he needed help. Even so, "He was not going to let the cancer interfere with his goals," says Barbie Edwards, one of his oncology nurses. "He never complained. In fact, sometimes Patty would take me out of the room to tell me that he was sick the night before. He would never say so. He ran on sheer will and faith."

Sometimes Bob would bring his guitar to chemo and play for the nurses. On one occasion, he gave Barbie a pair of hockey sticks. He wanted to be doing for others, even as he knew he was dependent on them. "If there was a happy thought to be had, he would find it," Barbie says. "When he finished chemo, he'd go back to work. Most people are just exhausted."

Bob would not let the disease or the treatment dictate the terms of his life. Growing up with a mother who never let hardship get her down gave Bob the tools to handle bad times. He always knew what so many people never learn—that you can't wait for happiness or optimism to *happen* to you. You'll be happy when you invest your time in making others happy. You'll be optimistic when you discover through your own actions that you can make positive changes in the world around you. Behavior is the key to attitude.

At the cancer center, they never mention statistics or calculate the odds, because, as Barbie Edwards says, "It's people like Bob who change the statistics. He had an aura about him; it just stayed with you even when he left."

Cancer has a way of grabbing your attention. I think one reason medical oncologists stay so positive is that for every person who gives up there's another who grows from the experience by learning how much he or she depends on others. With cancer, you discover how small and powerless you are; you also discover how much people love you and how your example can give them hope. That's why people were drawn to Bob when he was sick: His optimism was reassuring proof that human beings can rise above any adversity.

When he finished his radiation and then chemo, Bob refocused on McQuaid and on making the CD of his songs that he'd been putting off for years. As development director, he was responsible for the annual appeal to alumni—a perfect fit for him. He had the contacts, and making the calls on his former students helped him sustain his network. He missed teaching, but he didn't want to get too close to the students and make his death—should he lose the tug of war—even harder on them. He kept charge of his life; he did not turn the decisions over to anyone else.

But I Write Songs

O f course Bob Schwartz had to make a CD of his songs. I got that part right away. As a writer, I know the feeling. I too want some of my words to survive me, to mean something to someone long after I am gone. Perhaps that is why I am writing this book.

As good a teacher as Bob was, it is not surprising that he turned to song to get his message across. A good teacher uses every tool at his or her disposal, and if music is one of them it is going to get used. But I would bet cash money that Bob also wrote songs as a way to add to his legacy, to be sure that he could leave behind something that his children could point to—just as architects can point to buildings they designed or lawmakers can point to bills they wrote.

The desire to matter after we die is a powerful motivator. If we can leave something solid, substantial, physical behind—even if it is only our words—it's as if we somehow escape mortality or survive our own death, even if it is in a small way.

Now, this raises a serious religious question, especially for us Catholics. In many ways, we have been taught that being remembered is of no consequence, that what those who come after us think of us has nothing to do with the disposition of our souls—and that is what *really matters*.

Once we are gone, who's to say we will even be conscious of how we are remembered? And if we are in the presence of God, why would we care how our songs or words or buildings or bills are regarded? And if we are *not* in the presence of God, will it matter that people on this side of eternity have favorable memories of us?

Live well in this life and God will reward us in the next. That is what we say we believe. But it is not so easy to think this way when we are looking at the end of this life the way Bob Schwartz was doing.

Despite the theological issues, however, the impulse to leave something behind is not all bad. It can spur us to do good things. We have a need to give, and leaving something behind is a way to give. Bob's songs were worth passing along, and making the CD was more than legacy-building; it was a project to live for, a way to buy time by setting goals.

In the year after Bob's death, I listened to his songs over and over again, searching for insights into the man—insights I could not have discerned in the whirlwind-rekindled friendship we shared for eighteen months.

Bob was a pure romantic. He didn't care about money; he didn't care about his clothes; he didn't care about climbing a career ladder. He was an idealist who was drawn to music for its power and for the lifestyle. He was attracted to fellow musicians who cultivated excess and eccentricity in order to experience life to the fullest, learn from their mistakes, and write songs about the entire process.

Bob did the same. His was a life lived fully—no looking back, no regrets. Whenever things went badly—or well, for that matter—Bob just wrote another song and made the events a part of his life story. He didn't talk much about his disappointments and fears—let alone his impending death. He let his songs do the talking. To better understand Bob, one would have to look at his songs. The music was a reflection of his inner strength and an open door to his spirit. His song *But I Write Songs* is all about finding strength in weakness:

> Been a lot of places, wish I'd never gone
> Been a lot of times, wish I'd said, "I'm wrong"
> Been a lot of things, wish I'd never said
> Woke a lot of times and wished I was alone in bed

> *Chorus*
> But I write songs. I wrote 'em before you
> I write songs, and this one's for you
> I write songs, I wrote 'em before you
> I write songs, and this one's for you.

> Could never take a picture that didn't turn out bad
> Could never tell a story that didn't end up sad
> Never took a drink without takin' one too many
> Made myself some money, haven't saved a penny

> Chased a pile of memories, even caught a few
> Did a little work I thought no one else could do
> Gave away some gifts—didn't mean—didn't even want to
> Now I mean to give you the melody I'm on to.

There is something freeing about acknowledging our weakness: Once it's on the table, we can move beyond it. For example, I admire good reporters who know how to find out who said what and when, who can knock on the doors of grieving relatives and make them feel good about sharing their memories of a homicide victim, who can identify and track down slumlords who've long ago moved out of state. I can't do any of that well. I know that, and by admitting it to myself I was able to move on to areas I am better at—first writing editorials and then opinion columns. I am a better analyzer than I am detective, and I'm a better man for being able to admit it.

Bob's CD, titled *Long Time Comin'*, "wound up being a palette for his life," says Tony Gross, who produced Bob's one and only CD at his recording studio. Finally putting the songs together in a permanent collection was a way for Bob to tie that life together.

Many of the songs were written years before Bob's cancer, but they reflect a life spent thinking about mortality and the capriciousness of day-to-day events. I've heard Bob's songs so often now that they've become a part of me. I feel the words are in some ways mine, yet they are obviously much more a part of Bob. When you write a song, you play with the words over and over; you listen for nuance and cadence; you wrestle with how they'll sound, with what meaning or image listeners will take from them. The act of composing lyrics that say just what you want to say must be wrenching for the songwriter, but the struggle eventually yields self-understanding. When Bob got cancer, he already had his battle plan in his head: He just lifted it from his songs.

In the song *The Last Jump*, for instance, he captures not just the fear of the unknown that death represents, but forgiveness and redemption as a son reconciles with the memory of his dead father:

> *The door opens wide*
> *To the darkness outside*
> *You circle around*
> *So far from the ground*
> *And hook up a line*
> *And pray one more time*
> *And you want to say "no"*
> *To the last jump*
>
> *No mission's complete*
> *Til you land on your feet*

You hit and you run
And wait for the sun
Then look 'round to see
Who's made it with me
Who's made it and taken
Their last jump

Chorus:
But you just don't say "no"
To the last jump
It's the one you've trained for
For all time
Into the black
With no turning back
And no telling what you may find

It's hard keeping friends
So close to the end
One minute you care
The next no one's there
Don't judge me too hard
If I kept up my guard
It was hard
Lovin' close to the last jump

Bob's father, John, had been a paratrooper in World War II. Bob wrote the song after John's death after he learned some important family history. At John Schwartz's wake, Vicki Bida noticed a small display next to the coffin with some of his war memorabilia, including copies of *A Bridge Too Far* and *The Longest Day*, both written by the Irish-American historian Cornelius Ryan.

"I asked some of John's friends about the books, and they said those were his favorites," Vicki says. "So I told them that Cornelius Ryan was my father, and they were very impressed and excited." Later, Vicki wondered if John had been one of the many veterans interviewed in preparation for Ryan's books. She checked, and sure enough, John Schwartz had completed a questionnaire for Ryan while the author was researching his 1974 novel, *A Bridge Too Far*.

On that form and during a separate interview for a veterans group, Bob's father said he'd signed on as a paratrooper in June 1942 after a sergeant came through the downtown Rochester recruitment office offering $50 a month in bonus pay to anyone who would agree to join up. "I was in love and I thought I could use the extra money, so I said, 'Sign me up,'" John Schwartz wrote.

In the interview, Schwartz described his first jump over Sicily. "At night, yes. It was a good thing that...they got us over the land. Some of [the paratroopers] landed in the Mediterranean, some of the pilots weren't too good navigators, but some of us were lucky."

Once on the ground, the jumpers joined the infantry until they were needed for another jump.

John was part of the bloody Waal River Crossing in September 1944. He parachuted into Holland on the 17th. And then, on the 20th, took part in the mission to capture the north end of the bridge at Nijmegen, Holland—described in great detail in *A Bridge Too Far*. The first wave of paratroopers to cross the raging Waal was cut in half by enemy fire and the swift current. But 200 men made it ashore and seized the bridge, driving the German army back.

John Schwartz, who was slightly wounded in the leg by a piece of shrapnel, didn't dramatize or embellish his account of those days, but it's clear from what he did say that the battle was as horrific as Ryan portrays it in his book.

Once they crossed the Waal and slipped into the woods, "Some Jerries were calling they wanted to surrender. We went out, and soon four or five of them came up out of the darkness toward us. After thoroughly searching them, we asked if there were any more of them down by the river. The soldiers said yes, so we started to call in German to come out with their hands up, and soon they started to come in. We were surprised at the number and very glad that they decided to surrender and not to fight."

Bob got a clear sense of what it must have been like to be one false step—or one good enemy shot—from death.

A few days later, John recalled that he and his lieutenant were collecting dead American soldiers and bringing them to a school. Then, while they were drinking coffee, "we heard a loud explosion. Going outside we saw several children lying around on the ground. Several were dead and several wounded. One boy about seven, with his leg severed below the knee, kept calling for his mother. It seemed that one of the children had gotten hold of a German grenade and accidentally exploded it."

John Schwartz talked often about the war to his children. But it was after his dad's death—and through the Vicki Bida connection—that Bob acquired the interviews and learned the full story. Bob got a clear sense of what it must have been like to be one false step—or one good enemy shot—from death, especially so close to the end of one's tour of duty. On one level, that's what *The Last Jump* is all about: the fear of death and the unknown, with the fear subdued only with determination and the support of one's friends.

The song, I think, may also have been an apology. The words, "Don't judge me too hard; if I kept up my guard; It was hard lovin' close to the last jump," seemed to excuse Bob's father's distance, his drinking, his indirection, his inability to say, "I love you." It was Bob forgiving, able to accept the weakness in his father as he battled his own weakness.

The CD was a microcosm of Bob's life, but it was not a simple production. First because Bob was not an experienced studio musician, and second because the lead singer had cancer.

Normally, a skilled producer such as Tony Gross works with the whole band, devising a plan and a structure for each cut. But with Bob, Tony had to improvise. He had no clue how long Bob would survive, so it was important to record his parts first. Tony jokes that it was like building a cake underneath the icing. "I used his existing arrangements," he says, "recording the songs as he had played them over the years at various places."

Bob had trouble keeping a steady beat. So the backup musicians (often friends of Bob's, also with little studio experience) who came in to lay down tracks had to mimic Bob's timing. "They had to be one with his heart and soul," Tony says.

The CD took about 250 hours of studio time to make. "A lot of that was sifting through parts of tracks, cleaning things up, and putting tracks together," Tony recalls. "There was never time to prepare. Bob would call and say, 'I'm feeling good today and just ran into so-and-so. He'll play the harp.' Then they'd come over and lay it down."

So it was messy, but a joy for Tony, a McQuaid alum. "Even in school, Bob never made you feel like a subordinate," he insists. "He always made you feel like an equal. I felt honored to do something for him. I've seen plenty of death, but this was different. I had an elderly guitar teacher. He was my musical mentor. When he got cancer, he never asked for anything, but I could have recorded him. I didn't because I was too intimidated. Bob was a second chance for me. To be able to do something for someone like him—I'll have it with me forever."

Bob's death was difficult, but not an unacceptable burden on his friends and family. It was an opportunity to give. It was also an opportunity to see and experience dying in a different way. Just being there, being present for Bob—as he had been present all his life for others— was the most important thing any of us could do.

I never thought Bob had much of a shot at beating the cancer, but I gradually began to see that just as cancer had made Bob a better person it was teaching me to be more patient and compassionate. There was no way to know how long Bob's death would take—or if, by some chance, he'd miraculously recover. But he was a constant reminder to accept that which we cannot change and to enjoy even the tiniest of victories.

Through his whole ordeal, Bob's songs could speak when he could not—or would not. The last verse of *I Gave You Each Other* is a bequest to his friends. He knows that he will have to let go, but he doesn't want to. He doesn't even know how to. Still, he knows that life will go on without him:

> *What about the ones who are left behind?*
> *Thinking they can't handle life that's truly been unkind*
> *Well, I don't give you more than you can stand*
> *And if you hold together then you'll hold a million hands.*

That verse is a perfect synopsis of Bob's faith: God doesn't give us more than we can stand, and if we stick together we can handle anything. The song also expresses Bob's wish that his passion for life would survive him through his friends.

I find that since my brief time with Bob before his death, I am more alert to acts of goodness that would have slipped right by me before. In the fall of 2002, I came across such a story and wrote about it in my newspaper column. A year earlier, an eighteen-year-old man from a town near Rochester was sentenced to prison for criminally negligent homicide. He had helped his seventeen-year-old girlfriend purchase drugs and then helped her inject what turned out to be a fatal dose of heroin.

In prison, the young man was diagnosed with aplastic anemia, a rare but fatal blood disease. The prosecutor in the case and the girlfriend's parents—devastated at the loss of their child—quickly agreed that he should be released and allowed to die at home.

It was a simple act of mercy, which is usually mistaken for going soft. In my column, I cited Shakespeare's line that mercy "is the gentle rain from heaven," but I added the next lines, which are even more powerful: "It is an attribute to God himself: And earthly power doth then show likest God's, when mercy seasons justice."

I wrote that "mercy lets us see the humanity in those who have robbed us of what matters most. Mercy enables us to surrender our resentment—not to forget injustice, but to *forgive* it."

It's not that Bob saw goodness that was invisible to others; he chose to *search* for the good in people, and so he found it. The reason I am so taken with Bob Schwartz's story is that I discovered his approach to life is also my own—choosing the rosier forecast. It is, I find, a matter of choosing to look at those human attributes that will renew my faith, rather than at those that will shake my trust in God and in other people.

Throughout the summer and fall of 1997 and into early 1998, the CD was Bob's most effective cancer treatment. It kept him connected to the people and the ideals he cared most about—and that helped him keep the cancer in its place.

The CD was a time machine. Every hour he gave to it, Bob was transported back to a time before cancer, to the place and time and reason he wrote each set of lyrics.

Still, he was always looking for new goals, hoping (if not believing) that God would not take him in the middle of a project. Hoping that as long as he had a purpose he would continue to be alive.

The release of the CD was accompanied by a big party at the club Milestones and several performances by Bob and his "band." Bob wanted to title the CD, "Bob Schwartz Live! (If You Buy It Right Now)." It was very funny, but it also showed that Bob could feel the enemy within advancing on his gut. His friends intervened to suggest a more conventional title. Only people who knew him, we said, would get the joke. Others would think he was nuts, or sick, or both. He relented, but with a trace of sadness. He hated to lose a funny line just because it might be considered in bad taste.

He did insist on printing up souvenir T-shirts that read: Bob Schwartz's Farewell Tour. "If you can't make fun of cancer, what can you make fun of?" he mused.

Those Miles

In the summer of 1997, John Denver did a show near Rochester and Bob Schwartz went to see his old friend with some mild apprehension. He didn't want to be pitied.

After the show, Denver greeted Bob and Patty warmly: "As I live and breathe, it's Bob Schwartz." As soon as John spoke, Bob was fine. The two were not close friends, but they did have a longtime connection. Kris O'Connor, Denver's road manager, never quite understood the connection, but he knew it was real: "I only had to be told once that Bob had backstage clearance. John always welcomed him, and Bob had complete access whenever he'd come to a show."

Bob wanted things to be that night as they always were—upbeat and all about the music, not about cancer and dying. Denver did not disappoint.

A month later, Bob spoke with Denver for the last time. Denver was in Houston for a show and Bob was being evaluated at the Stehlin Institute. They stayed in the same hotel, met for drinks, and Bob and Patty went to the concert. Denver showed them pictures of the plane he was about to buy.

Two weeks later, John Denver, fifty-three years old, crashed his Long-EZ experimental two-seat plane into Monterey Bay, not far from Pacific Grove, California. It was a big news story, but to Bob, John's untimely death was also a reminder that life is fragile and unpredictable, and it came at a moment when Bob desperately wanted stability and predictability. Back in the summer, he had been able to draw on Denver's energy and hope. Suddenly, it was all gone.

When Denver's plane crashed, Bob went down too. Hard. And he didn't get up quickly. Friends and family, knowing of his connection to Denver, sent him newspaper and magazine stories about the singer's death. He saved them all.

Bob had hoped that Denver would help him produce the CD of his songs. Through his friendship with Denver, he felt connected to a world bigger than Rochester and McQuaid. With Denver's death, Bob's world got smaller—even as he was trying to fight the cancer by expanding his circle of friends.

I sensed what Bob was going through. I expected that Denver's death would be devastating for Bob. But I didn't pick up the phone when I read of the plane crash. Just as when I read the account of his cancer, I did not know what to say. Bob was not going to get over this; time would not heal this wound; life would not get back to normal.

I am not proud of what I didn't do. We Catholics pray at Mass for forgiveness for what we have done and "for what we have failed to do." This was a perfect example of what we call a "sin of omission." But I think this failure on my part has finally taught me that it is precisely in those awkward moments, when the pain is deep and the fear is overpowering, that it is most important to pick up the phone. It doesn't matter what you say; it only matters that you care.

Just as when we first reconnected, it was Bob who called me. It is nice to have a friend who understands his own embarrassing lapses well enough to accept them in others—no questions asked. He was more determined than ever to make his CD and keep working. For every connection he lost, he made another. He found one reason after another to go on.

One day, he spoke to Jeff Van Gundy, then the head coach of the New York Knicks of the National Basketball Association. Van Gundy, a former Rochesterian, had earlier been coach of the McQuaid Knights. Bob floated an idea for Van Gundy's reaction: What if NBA team planes could make seats available to cancer patients who needed to travel for treatment—much as many corporations let patients fly along on company planes? Van Gundy gave him some names and numbers to try.

"What do you think?" he asked me. "Give it a try," I said. "It might work, and it can't hurt."

Bob did pursue the idea on and off for months, but without any success—just some polite promises to look into it. Eventually, he gave up, when it suddenly hit him that the NBA might not want private citizens getting a close-up look at players not always known for being on their best behavior. That may not have been the reason at all. It might have been just completely impractical—a logistical challenge that would require having patients connect with one team plane after another, on very tight schedules, to make it to wherever they were slated for treatment. Who knows?

So Bob eventually put this idea aside and moved on. He had no time to waste on dead ends.

At about the same time, early in 1998, the cancer began to spread again. Dr. Garrow thought it made sense to buy as much time as possible with a second round of chemo with a newer drug, Gemcitabine.

Bob gladly took the treatment, but cancer can quickly become resistant to the drug, and Bob's had.

He continued with the treatment anyway. A few times, I drove him to and from the cancer center and waited with him while the Gemcitabine dripped slowly into his system. There were good days and bad during this phase. The day after a treatment, he was generally up and feeling good; on the second and third days, he was typically sick. So like all cancer patients, he began to plan his schedule around the treatment—staying clear of commitments on days he knew would be bad ones. He didn't like conceding anything to cancer, not even the inevitability of a bad day, but the chemo was another way to keep him focused on the road ahead. He used it to his advantage.

All he wanted for his birthday was time.

In early May, days before his fiftieth birthday—May 4—Bob developed a blood clot near the catheter Dr. Chang had inserted in his neck to facilitate the chemo. A big bash had been planned for Bob's half-century gala. He was looking forward to it. It would have been another chance to laugh in cancer's face. But it wasn't to be. Cancer got the last laugh this time.

I went to see him at the Genesee Hospital. He was in an intensive care unit; some friends and family had camped out in a waiting room, where they could have food and drinks and birthday cake—none of which was permitted in Bob's ICU room.

At least a couple of patients in ICU had died the night before, and Bob was semi-awake as their bodies were wheeled to the elevators. "It's a great place to be," he said. "I was voted by the other patients as most likely to make it through the night."

"The good news," he told me, "is that they think they can dissolve the clot. The bad news was that they had to take out the catheter, and since I had already eaten lunch they couldn't use anesthesia. That's something I'd rather not go through again."

A clot was not unusual. And while it would have been fatal had it traveled into his lungs, it did not. Dr. Chang put Bob on Coumatin, a blood thinner, and the clot eventually dissolved.

Still, those were very dark days. Bob was as depressed as I had seen him. He tried to hide it, but he could not. Not even the kidding around could mask his deep disappointment. He desperately wanted to be at the party. It would have been another powerful message to himself that he was still living a normal life, doing normal things. It would have been another chance to soak in the energy of friends and family. To spend that night in the hospital was to swallow another setback.

All he wanted for his birthday was time. And he was discovering that without the expectation of time it was very hard to pull himself along. He sat propped up in the hospital bed, looking out the window at an overcast sky. "People make plans. That's what we do," he said. "I don't know how to plan for *no* future. I don't know how much time I have. I set goals to keep myself positive, but I just don't know what I'm working with."

I had never thought of it that way, and I had no response. We sat for a few moments in silence. There was nothing I could do except be present to my friend. I couldn't change anything or make him feel better. Eventually I got up to leave and promised to call in a day or two. Bob nodded and fixed his eyes on the ceiling.

Bob had a song for just such a moment. Like the others, it had become a script for his final days. *Half a Hundred Years* was a tribute to many of the priests he had known over the years. Its author hungers for more time and struggles to accept God's will:

Half a hundred years in the service of the Lord
Half a hundred more would be my reward
But whatever you wish for me
I accept willingly

Casting fire on the earth, molding minds, building men
This I did in your name and would gladly again
But whatever you wish for me
I accept lovingly

I am a priest forever
According to Your plan

In the presence of Your Holy Mother
I renew all my vows again

Half a hundred years in the service of the Lord
Half a hundred more would be my reward
But whatever You wish for me
I accept lovingly, I accept willingly
I accept lovingly.

Whenever I read or listen to those lyrics, I think of Bob that day at the hospital. There is nothing easy about faith. We are taught at an early age to love life, our own and that of others, to protect it, to fight for it. And yet we are reminded of Jesus' words in Gethsemane—"Not My will, but Yours be done."

Just knowing God's will is hard enough. Accepting it—if it means death—is the most difficult test of all. Bob wanted half a hundred years more—or even ten or twenty more—and he didn't believe God would give him more pain or defeat than he could handle. That meant holding on to life and fighting every impulse to self-pity. "I accept, willingly," he wrote.

But how do you learn the difference between *giving up* and *accepting the inevitability* of death so that you may experience it fully—as the portal to another phase of life? How do you know when fighting is just futile? How do you stop resisting the natural impulse to fight for your life? And the biggest question of all: Should you ever give up?

I don't think Bob ever fully answered those questions for himself. I don't know that any of us can. But he had an approach. "When the doctor says to me, 'You've got three months,' I say, 'Don't tell me what the book says. I'm Bob. I'm me.' Maybe I have longer than that. And so far, I've been a better judge of me than the doctors. I'm just going to stay positive and take whatever time I can."

Bob chose to hang on. Dying doesn't come with a set of Cliffs

Notes. And that's why we have to trust the person we've become—the person we've constructed from hard decisions and experience. We have to do what seems right for us, do what our heart and our head tell us to do.

While Bob always rejected any comparisons to the late Cardinal Joseph Bernardin—who, at the age of sixty-eight, publicly came to terms with his own death from cancer—there are similarities in their circumstances. Bernardin, who died in 1996, put his death on display, as did Bob. Even as he knew that death is the door to eternal life, he feared it, had doubts of faith, and struggled with excruciating pain. So too did Bob Schwartz.

In the final month of his life, Bernardin, the archbishop of Chicago, sent early Christmas cards to priests and other friends. Shortly after his death, *Time* magazine reported, "His parting to those who came to say good-bye was to squeeze their hand, asking with his eyes that they walk his final journey with him." Bob invited people to walk his final walk with him, but he never—*ever*—said good-bye.

As Bob was dying, I found myself thinking more and more about pain. My life has been quite free of pain. I've never spent a night in the hospital, never had a broken bone, and never had a chronic illness. How do people learn to deal with pain? How do they ignore it? How do they find a way to make something else dominate their consciousness? The answer is that something in your life has to be so powerful that it can push the pain far out of your mind. Obviously, people can learn to do this. Bob learned. He didn't want to lose who he was— teacher, father, husband, friend—to the pain, so he never let himself give in to the pain. Every waking moment, he was who he was.

Bob was offering a preview of the journey we will all take. While private, quiet prayer and reflection came naturally to Cardinal Bernardin, it did not come naturally to Bob. His prayer was in his relationships; doing good work was his offering to God. He did not find comfort in quiet contemplation. Of course he thought about matters of life and death all the time, and he was hot-wired to see delicious ironies all about. His songs and his parables testify to a very active mind. But he turned outward—not inward—to find himself and understand his place in the world.

Bob's simple kindness was his prayer, not the *fruit* of his prayer. For him, action was spirituality. He could only pray and set himself right with God by reaching out to others when he was sick—even more so than when he was healthy. The sicker he got, the more he needed the contact with other people. In his friends, he was looking for the face of God. He could not die alone, for to do so would be to die without the hope that would carry him to the other side.

Obviously, his sense of place in the larger community—in the Communion of Saints—was real and important. I want that same awareness, but I want a spiritual life that provides me a place within my soul—a quiet place where I can go in times of trouble, where I can listen for God. I cannot say that Bob had no such place of his own, although it was never apparent to me. What matters is that we all find ways to move closer to God. Bob found his way, and since Bob's death I have started to find mine. I find myself more often retreating to private prayer.

I did call Bob a couple of days after our encounter in the hospital as I had promised him, but early May was the start of another baseball season for my two boys. We spent nearly every night and parts of the weekend at the fields, so my contacts with Bob fell off a bit for a few weeks.

It was during this time that I began to think about writing Bob's story. Patty had offered me the Tupperware tubs full of cards and letters, and at night, after the games and the kids' bedtime, I began to read through the stacks of greetings and long letters that had been accumulating in the Schwartz's garage.

In those plastic tubs was proof that each life is like a pebble thrown into a pond—rippling concentric circles in all directions, reaching far from home. Some correspondence was from people who did not know Bob at all but had heard about his situation. I was curious about dozens of letters and cards decorated with pictures of pigs (dancing, eating, strutting). The Pig Lady was Nancy Saddock, a Rochester native who had long ago moved to Hartford, Connecticut.

Her sister in Rochester sent Nancy an article from the *Democrat and Chronicle* on John Denver's impact on local fans. Nancy Saddock was also a Denver fan. She read about Bob, who was featured in the story, and sent him a letter at McQuaid asking for the title of a Denver song she couldn't remember. Bob had the answer, and a few weeks later, when she was visiting her sister, Nancy went over to meet him. Bob made her tapes of albums she didn't have. "It was like we'd known him forever," Nancy recalls. On her few visits with him, Nancy concluded that "he never forgot anything anyone ever said. It was like he was never sick. He was always happy to see us."

Bob Schwartz never missed an opportunity to expand his network; human contact was as powerful as chemotherapy for him.

Some letters were more than kind greetings. One in particular made me keenly aware of Bob's very special connection to the people who had passed through his life. It was an eleven-page, handwritten testament from a former student who had gone on to college and graduate school, eventually earning a Ph.D. It was a chronology of a young man's search for meaning and truth, a gift he was able to share with a teacher now struggling himself to hold on to meaning and truth. It was filled with revelations of disappointments and doubts, with references to God and faith and the uncertainty of it all. At the end, the former student wrote, "As I said, I don't pray very well, but I will think of you…. Perhaps I shall return to academic life someday. But in the meantime, it's good to know there are people like you around. And I am very glad, and quite proud, that you were once my teacher."

The letter made me think of the parable of the One-Point Rule (inspired by Bob's high school friend who was killed in Vietnam). I'm sure Bob had told this student that story, with its punch line—"If you ever need a point, just ask. Grading is not an exact science."

I wondered if the letter was a belated plea for that one additional point, for a passing grade in life. I do not know. But as I sifted through the Tupperware tubs, I grew more confident that the story of Bob's honest death should be told. His story is as old as time and as new as each dawn: We reap what we sow. He pushed his students to know themselves, to live by faith, to be there for others—and the seeds he planted became sweet fruit. In those cards and letters, the harvest was bountiful.

In late August, we agreed that I would try to write this book, although at the time I wasn't sure what exactly it would be about. Bob loved the idea. He saw it as another goal, something left to be accomplished. So he and I agreed we'd talk by phone or in person as often as possible, for whatever time he had left. And so we did.

From there on, over the last two and a half months of his life, Bob and I talked. He could no longer hold back the cancer by the sheer force of his will. The scouting party had grown into an enormous army of cancer cells, attacking on several fronts. Bob's resolve didn't falter, but his body did.

Wednesdays and Thursdays were his worst days because of the Monday chemo. He was worried that the morphine might be making the discomfort worse, but he wasn't sure.

"We went to dinner last night," he said. "Patty woke me up. I really wanted to sleep, but I don't want people to think I have an automatic out. I am married to this cancer now. And I am going to have to live with it. Emphasis on *live*."

He decided to go to Tony Gross' studio to record a song he had written in memory of friendship with John Denver. I went with him because I thought it might be fun to see how it was done, but the whole thing was hard to watch.

Bob was exhausted before he started to record. He was looking gray and weak. He kept rubbing his stomach to ease the pain. But he had to do it. He had to finish this gift he had written for a friend who wasn't supposed to have died before he did.

With each take, Bob's voice got a little softer, a little more distant. But he kept at it. He said he didn't want to waste Tony's time, "So I found a way to do a good take." (In fact, Tony later had to patch together parts of two or three takes to get a usable one.)

It was nearly a year after John Denver's death, but the sadness of it hadn't faded for Bob: "When John called me in June of 1997, there was so much emotion in his voice. He wanted me to be well, but I felt he was having trouble communicating that to me over the phone."

That call was the basis for the lead to *I Called You Friend*:

> *I called you friend; You called me then*
> *We cried out loud; And tried somehow*
> *To make sense*
> *Of being friends*
>
> *We traveled back those thirty years*
> *Success is not what it appears*
> *You had it all*
> *It didn't fit*
> *I had it bad*
> *But couldn't quit*

And later:

> *You worried way too much for you*
> *And shared what you were going through*
> *I swore that I would be all right*
> *You asked how you could share my fight*
>
> *You gave me hope to realize that good friends*
> *Can tell each other lies*
> *You made some plans*
> *They half came true*
> *You died before I could sing for you.*

Friends can tell each other lies. Of course they can. Not the destructive, killing kind of lie, but lies of omission—the ones we tell to lift each other up. When Bob last saw Denver, he didn't want to talk about cancer; he wanted to talk about the music. Denver obliged. He was not unaware of the devastation cancer was causing in Bob's gut. He just chose to give his friend what he needed—a sense of normalcy. You don't tell a guy like Bob, "Give it up; you can't beat this." You tell him that anything can happen. You encourage him to live as long and as well as he can.

As much as Bob wanted to be there for others, however, by the end of summer the roles had reversed. Bob's people—his fellow paratroopers—were there for him. He needed reassurance. And he would have it.

At some point—always a hard point to spot exactly—the rosier forecasts we choose to believe are no longer powerful enough to keep us from admitting that storm clouds are gathering. Bob thought he could keep being there for his family and friends if he could continue his daily rituals—even things as simple as making the morning coffee or burning newspapers in the fireplace. It worked for a while.

He knew that as long as he could make jokes, he could make it easier for people to see him. There would be no tears, no moping, no self-pity—not in public, not ever. And he would let his struggle, like his CD, be part of his legacy—a message to everyone who knew him.

"Cancer dictates; I'm just the stenographer," he told me one day. Bob saw everything in terms of victory or defeat. The more victories, however small, the better he felt. Recording that last song for John Denver was a win.

A day after the night in the studio, he decided to stop taking the Coumadin. "I don't think I need it, and I'd like to get rid of at least one of the drugs going into my body," he told Patty. "It's a small victory, but I need small victories."

Even as I watched Bob die, freighted with more pain every day, fighting it every step of the way, I was convinced his story would, finally, be about a good death, about a man's coming to terms with dying and accepting it. But we have been so conditioned to believe that to die right—to die with dignity—means an orderly passing. Once we understand that we're not going to make it, we're supposed to accept it and begin shutting down. We're supposed to say our good-byes, make sure our affairs are in order, and go to sleep. If the pain is great, or if our care is a burden on those around us, we're supposed to step aside. We are to go *quietly*, for somehow that means we are going with *dignity*. Sometimes we actually think we can call the shots, that we can declare ourselves "ready to die" and then, well, just die. But life and death are not so simple. And acceptance is not the main theme of Bob's story. It took me two years after his death to figure that out, so powerful is our desire to script life as if it were a Broadway play.

The truth is, his was a hard death. And pain did change Bob's outlook. When he first started with morphine pills, they kept his pain under control. "If this is as bad as it gets," he told me, "I can deal with it. The morphine is great."

But by mid-August, he was talking about working around the pain where possible, conceding that it had begun to take control. He stopped talking about surviving.

"I don't think he's in denial," Patty said. "He just doesn't want anyone around him to see him giving up."

He joked one day about a parody of the movie, "My Dinner with Andre." Gemcitabine, he said, "is starring in a new movie called, 'My Dinner *is* Bob.'"

One day, he complained of an "absolutely horrible day, pain wise. This is the cancer pain people go through. I never realized it could be so bad. The morphine doesn't touch it. I can almost understand how somebody would say, 'Put me under.' And I can see a doctor doing it with a clear conscience."

He said he could *almost* understand. He would regularly joke about calling Dr. Kevorkian. But he never gave it serious thought. You don't give up on life, he would say. You regroup and come right back.

I think the fear of giving up kept him from giving up. Depending on how you saw him, he was incredibly strong or incredibly needy—not weak of character or faith but terrified of losing those he loved.

He dealt with the pain; it was "the black" he feared. At one point, with pain he likened to "an ice cream headache in my chest," he wound up back at the hospital. "I had a mug of cold water, and then I was still so hot I sweated right through my shirt. I could hardly stand up."

Even so, when he got to the emergency room, he refused a rectal exam. He didn't think he needed it. And saying no felt like a small victory. He was making choices…while he still could.

So it was a no-brainer when Kris O'Connor called to ask Bob to sing a song in Aspen in October during a memorial tribute to John Denver. Bob didn't care about the pain; Kris' request was both an opportunity to salute his friend and a compliment. He said yes without hesitation.

And he said yes, too, to the Bluebird Café in Nashville, where he'd played earlier in the summer. In June, when he sang, he told the crowd about his cancer and his determination to fight it, and the audience cheered him warmly. The Bluebird asked him to come back the last weekend in September to play at a Songwriter's Showcase evening. Prepping for a performance was better medicine

Bob did worry about being too heavy a burden for his family.

for his pain than any amount of morphine.

Of course, he never made either appearance.

For those last months, the Schwartz home was as it always had been—full of people. From time to time, Patty would play traffic cop, asking people to stay away or at least to give the four of them a little time together alone as a family. But there was no real privacy. Bob's Farewell Tour moved to his living room (later it would move to his bedroom), his friends trying desperately to comfort him and learn from him at the same time.

Bob did worry about being too heavy a burden for his family. He confided to Mike O'Leary—his former student and owner of Milestones, the bar where Bob played regularly in his last year—that he was afraid that his being at McQuaid would be tough on Eric. Bob thought school should be a place where kids can escape outside stresses in their lives.

The truth is, he *was* a burden. Caring for him was at times difficult and exasperating, but I never observed anyone close to him ever resenting it. He required intense devotion, constant vigilance, and boundless patience—especially on his bad days.

I (and I was not the only one) was trying to decide whether witnessing Bob's ordeal up close was a gift or a punishment. Did he really have lessons to teach us, or was he just stubbornly clinging to the remnants of a life that he could never get back?

These questions were, in a way, gifts—food for a lifetime of thought. My search for answers even to this day rightly focuses my mind on my soul, reminding me that the real purpose to this life is to prepare for the next. Here are some of the questions I ask myself (and the answers I am arriving at):

Does love require us to us to seek a death that is easy on family and friends? No. Of course good people will do what they can to avoid overloading the people they love, but sometimes the struggle to live is unavoidably hard on others. Life is often difficult and wearing, just as it is often unexpectedly joyous and exhilarating.

Does love allow us to ask family and friends to accept the burden of a painful death as a way to deepen our appreciation for the time we have? Yes. Of course it comes naturally only for those who, like Bob Schwartz, have lived their lives accepting the burdens others ask of them.

Are we just fooling ourselves when we think we can will or joke or pray ourselves back to good health? Probably. Of course all of us are going to die sometime, but optimism certainly can postpone the inevitable.

I would stop by to check on Bob on my lunch hour or after work. Usually we'd talk for a few minutes, depending on how he felt. I'd chat with Patty, or Vicki, or whoever happened to be around. Every night, I was amazed at Bob's grip on life. I hate the idea of assisted suicide or euthanasia, but I couldn't imagine waking up with that much pain at two in the morning and not begging God to take me. But I had learned that the sustenance Bob took from his relationships allowed him to displace the pain enough to hold on.

Given his intuitive sense of community and his faith, I am still surprised at Bob's aversion to formal church life. Oh sure, churches can be exasperating, heavy on bureaucracy, resistant to change, preoccupied with raising money. And in the Catholic Church these days, the child abuse and coverup scandals still loom large.

But churches are flawed by definition. They exist for sinners who come to church for refuge, for strength. Bob certainly understood this. He instinctively found the good in weak and sinful human beings. Why didn't he find more solace in a flawed church?

I think it was simply that Bob's friends were church for him.

As the summer of 1998 came to an end, the setbacks began to overtake the victories. Bob's struggle to keep all things as normal as possible failed.

He looked forward to full and busy days at McQuaid, but he didn't have the strength to maintain a regular schedule. He was lucky to have McQuaid, because the school was full of fellow paratroopers who were perfectly willing to do anything necessary to support Bob in his hour of need.

He took another hit in late August when Dr. Garrow ended his chemo. It wasn't doing Bob any good; it was just making him feel sicker. But to Bob, giving up the treatment was like an admission of failure. He wanted to stay with the Gemcitabine, if only to tell himself he was doing all he could—even though he knew that days two and three after the treatment were always horrific.

But there was no point to more chemo. The cancerous army was tightening the noose, closing in on all his vital organs. "Dr. Garrow is right," I said to Bob. "Maybe without the chemo, you'll feel better and be able to do some of the things you want to do."

"I hope so," he said. "But this sure feels wrong. I'm going to have to manufacture some good news."

There was no more hope for recovery, so it was really important for his family and friends to help Bob find other reasons to hope—not for a long cancer-free life but for a few good days during which he could still make a difference.

He began to wonder if he'd done the right thing sticking with the conventional course of treatment rather than running off to parts unknown in pursuit of something new and risky that might have turned out to be the miracle cure. If you're going to die anyway, why not die trying something new?

And then he'd come back to reality. He told me about the brother-in-law of a friend, who was diagnosed with cancer of the appendix in May. "He died last week," Bob said. "When he got the cancer he told me, 'I'm going for the cure. I'm going to beat this.' So he borrowed $2,000 from everybody in his family and went to Mexico to take Laetrile. I told Patty everything I've read about quack treatments and that [our strategy] (chemo and radiation) is the right therapy. I hope I'm not wrong."

He wasn't wrong, and not just because the miracle treatments wouldn't have worked. Bob would have been miserable racing off to some other part of the world to chase a pipe dream while giving up all the things that really mattered to him back home.

But like anyone who can see the final days, Bob was wondering if he could have done something else, if he had missed his only chance to survive. "I've seen people go all over the world looking for exotic treatments for cancer," says Bob's friend, Father Jim Schwartz (no relation). "It's very seductive. But Bob was well grounded. He was listening to his body and knew what to do. The doubts [at the end] were really a measure of his determination to use every ounce of energy he had to fight back."

Bob's cancer had scared his daughter Jenny from the moment it was diagnosed. That's one reason she was always trying to get out of the house to stay with friends. She just couldn't bear the thought of his dying. And there was nothing in her experience that prepared her for losing her father. She didn't know what she could do for Bob, and she didn't now how to cope with her own fear. I think a lot of us felt the same. We'd pull back from time to time to catch our breath, and then get back into that plane that was circling above the battlefield in the dark of night.

Jenny showed us all the way: Just hang in there; be there as much as possible; trust that your heart will lead you in the right direction.

Bob knew Jenny was scared and he wanted to arrange a time for the two of them to talk—maybe spend a night away from home at a hotel. They picked a date, but when it came Bob was too sick to leave the house. Instead, a few days later, Jenny came home one day feeling especially sad. She raced through the house to Eric's downstairs bed-room—so Bob wouldn't see her cry.

"Daddy came down and found me. I was trying to hide. But he sat down and said, 'I'm going to die. It's OK. You can cry if you want, or ask whatever you want.'" She hugged Bob, but fought back her tears. A few months earlier, she'd made Bob a hockey stick in art class, a real full size hockey stick that she cut herself on the jigsaw. She painted it McQuaid gold and black, and lettered it: "For Daddy, From Jenny." She was so proud of that stick, and Bob was touched right to his soul. It was her gift to Dad.

Now her gift was not crying. It was not time to say good-bye, and Jenny sensed that the kindest thing she could do for her father was not to show her true feelings, not to show him how scared she was and how much she would miss him. He wasn't showing his true feelings either, yet neither one of them was being dishonest. It was just as Bob had written in his farewell song to John Denver: "Good friends can tell each other lies." Jenny and Bob wanted the same thing: to put each other at ease and make each other comfortable, despite their own pain. That's the very definition of love. They wanted the best for each other, and they were stumbling to find what was best.

And I was stumbling right along with them.

You had to just hang on. Pray a little. Think a little. Listen a little. Bob's lifelines were disappearing. He found out that the John Denver tribute was overbooked and that he was off the program. "Nobody deserves to be there more than I do. But I'm sure Kris fought for me as hard as he could. I'm just going to have to come to grips with it. It was not meant to be."

Jenny knew the truth of it: "He was devastated. He was so pissed. He got his hopes up so high, and they were crushed. He was hurt, really hurt."

"Oh, something will happen," Bob said, dismissing his disappointment to make everyone else comfortable. "There could be a Denver concert here in Rochester on October 12. Or maybe I'll be in Houston then. I don't know. But things happen for a reason. I just don't know what it is yet."

I felt so bad for him. I too was angry. He was like a gutsy fighter, too stubborn to quit but unable to protect himself from the blows raining down on his head and body. It was so unfair. He was losing weight. His eyes were sad and sunken. He was always smiling, but even his jokes had taken on a sadder quality.

"When I got cancer, I wanted to live long enough to walk Jenny down the aisle," he would say. "Now I'm happy to have outlived Sinatra."

I knew how much Aspen meant. I didn't think that come October, he'd be able to make the trip, let alone perform (and, in fact, he could not have), but Bob was right—he deserved to be asked and to be there if possible.

"He was a good friend to John," says Kris O'Connor. "He never tried to push songs. He never picked up John's guitar and said, 'Hey, you've got to hear this.' He didn't impose. Friends don't do that. He was just a good person, and John appreciated that."

To Bob, singing at the Denver memorial was his last chance to be on the big stage, his last chance to salute his friend, and his last chance to show the world what he could do. He was selfless and self-effacing, but he was not without ego. He always wondered if he could have made it big—if the strength of his lyrics and the resonance of his themes would have overcome the weakness of his voice and guitar playing. But as with all his disappointments, Bob boxed this one up and put it away quickly. He had no time to dwell on it or let the sadness consume his time.

The stage was Bob's pulpit. And the performance aspect of teaching was part of its appeal. "As a teacher, you're always on," he said, "always performing. I've often wondered what that first year of retirement [from teaching] might be like—the withdrawal of it. After you've done it for thirty years—and you've got all this knowledge to impart—suddenly there's no one to impart it to."

The school year, like a baseball season, has a natural rhythm—a well-defined beginning, midyear, and ending. "There's constant renewal," Bob would say. "You learn to hang on for what's around the next bend. If you have a dull class, you hang on for the next one. It's good training for dealing with bad news—let's hang on and see what's next."

Bob was tenacious when it came to fighting for what mattered to him, but he was not a brooder—feeling sorry for himself when it became obvious that something he hoped for wasn't going to work out. The teacher in him knew there'd be another day, another school year, a fresh start.

On the Wednesday before Labor Day, one of Bob's cancer buddies from Genesee Hospital stopped to see him at McQuaid. "I hadn't called him in a while because I didn't have any good news for him," Bob said. "And his wife told me he hadn't called me for the same reason. He had that cancer look. He was yellow and thin, his eyes heavy. I had the feeling he was hugging me good-bye."

He was. Shortly after that day, his friend left to try a last-ditch treatment in California. He never returned. The cancer look reminded Bob how his friend Tom O'Neill had begun to prepare his wife Carol for the day he would no longer be there. Suddenly, Bob began to do likewise. "He showed Eric how to reset the breakers," Patty says, "and how to replace the furnace filters. He got Barry York to take care of our finances, he got another friend to take care of the pool, and he asked others to be available for simple home repairs."

And then there was The List. "He began to interview people he thought I might want to date," Patty remembers. "He was so controlling, even then. It was embarrassing." But it was funny, too, and endearing. It was Bob's way of saying, don't be afraid to move on without me—even though he wanted to hold on tight to Patty, Eric and Jen, hoping their energy could pull him back from the abyss.

You Just Can't Say No

Senior Day for the Class of 1999 was on the Friday of the first week of school, and the kids asked Bob Schwartz to say a few words in the chapel to kick off the day.

Teachers and students were bustling about the cafeteria before the day's events. Bob was standing alone at the food table, spreading cream cheese on half a bagel. He couldn't keep much down, but that didn't stop him from trying to eat. He took a couple of bites and had a few sips of orange juice. He didn't look like a motivational speaker. He was wearing a pair of khakis, well worn and shiny; a white dress shirt, threadbare, its collar covered with little nits from too many washes. It was loose around his neck. He wore a brown-patterned tie, Windsor-knotted but hanging free below an open collar.

His eyes kept darting around the room, and he couldn't seem to finish a thought. His mind was racing, recalling students who'd contemplated suicide. He was always devastated by kids, with their whole lives ahead of them, thinking about ending them.

"And here I am," he said in between bites. "I'd give anything to have my life ahead of me." As the seniors mugged and clowned around in the cafeteria that morning, Bob was still scrolling the cue cards in his mind, looking for the right words to say to them.

The chapel is a warm and inviting space, paneled in honey-toned oak. The sun streamed through the windows; excitement was in the air—as it always is when students are pumped for the start of a new adventure. Bob was introduced.

"In the last twenty months, I've twice been given three months to live," he told the boys. "The doctors were wrong. People will tell you things about yourself that you don't have to accept. You know yourself, and you know what you can accomplish. So always do your best. You can do great things, but you have to listen to your inner voice.

"Bob Dylan has a line—'If you're not busy being born, you're busy dying.' I'm going to be busy being born until you graduate." No one who saw him that morning believed Bob had ten more months to live, but the boys broke into a loud and sustained applause. They stood as one.

When they stopped cheering, Bob continued. "You have to keep moving forward toward graduation. That's what I keep doing—moving forward toward a new goal all the time."

Suddenly, one of the boys stood and asked for the floor. Bob ceded his time, and the young man came forward.

"When I leave school today, I'm going back to the hospital, to the psychiatric unit," he said. "I'm living there now. I know some of you tried to find me over the summer. I've had some problems—bipolar disease, they say. I don't believe that's what's wrong. But I have had a tough year. My father had me arrested because I was fighting him, and the police came and took me to the hospital. I'm going to beat this. I'm going to be all right. Mr. Schwartz is fighting, and so am I."

He stopped for a moment and then pointed to the crucifix over the altar. "Whenever you think nobody cares, take it to Him."

It was a remarkable moment in a long series of remarkable moments during Bob's journey with cancer. An adolescent baring his soul in public is rare. But it was a tribute to the honesty Bob always inspired in others by being honest himself. As he said, in teaching you hang on during the down times to see what's around the next bend—often you'll be pleasantly surprised. It was also clear that this young man trusted his classmates and—like Bob—was willing to lean on them to get through. He, too, had discovered the Communion of Saints.

Bob was amazed at the student's candor—and expression of hope. He actually got stronger as the morning wore on, buoyed by the enthusiasm and compassion of his son Eric and his classmates.

Still, for every ounce of sustenance Bob took from the students, the cancer took back two ounces. By early September, ten weeks before he died, Bob was getting just two to three hours of sleep because of the pain. Every night, "he's up and down like a jack-in-the-box," Patty said.

She was running on fumes, exhausted but unable to take a break from Bob. Friends volunteered to spend nights with him so that she could get some rest, but she wanted to get Bob into hospice care. She wanted someone to assume the responsibility for his medical care so she could just be his wife—so that she could cry if she felt like it and get out of the room when she needed a cigarette.

But Bob hated the idea of hospice. He didn't mind it for other people, but it was not for him. "It's like giving up, like admitting you're going to die," he said. It wasn't as if he could think clearly about this, however. He wanted to be at home, and he wanted things to be "normal," but his illness was increasingly burdensome to everyone.

Like his family, I wanted Bob to be happy. I knew that he needed the familiarity of home. I understood that the more choices he could leave for himself, the more alive he felt. Still, how could a guy whose whole life was given to acts of kindness, growing from a faith deep within, not surrender to God at the end? If he wanted to turn his battle with cancer into a lesson for his students, why didn't he talk about his internal struggle—the one to keep his faith despite what was happening to him? Why didn't he at least explain the conflict between letting go and holding on?

The answer is a contradiction, I'm afraid. Bob avoided hospice as a way to stop himself from crossing a certain bridge. He did not want to go from *knowing* he was dying to *acting* as if death were near. The finality of hospice bothered him, even as he was making The List of potential new husbands for Patty.

The compromise they finally arrived at was a home hospice nurse, introduced to Bob as an "enhanced care nurse." Patricia Duffy, a fifteen-year veteran of hospice care, started coming by daily. "She's going to mix the pain-killer cocktails for me," Bob said. He worked out a deal with McQuaid so that he could work from home—mostly making alumni solicitation calls and tending to the data bank of donors. In fact, Bob never made any calls, because he could barely talk. On the phone, his voice was no more than a whisper, and the "cocktail" of morphine, Ativan (the sedative), and Compazine (to inhibit nausea and vomiting) left him incoherent for hours on end.

On some days, Bob would sound almost like his old self. His voice would surge with energy for a brief conversation. Then the drugs would settle like fog in the valleys of his brain. He was mostly incoherent, but he struggled to control the pain enough to do those things he needed to do.

Whenever he could collect his thoughts, he kept on preaching to his kids to "be normal—go on with your life," but that wasn't really what he meant or wanted.

"Sometimes," he confided to me one night, "they are too normal. Eric comes home and says, 'When are we going to eat?' not 'How are you feeling?' Jenny says she was the hero at her soccer game and they carried her off the field 'and neither of you were there.' I asked them to live normally, but they pretend like I'm not sick. I don't want them to act like normal, selfish kids. That's not the *normal* I had in mind."

Teenagers as a group are just beginning to understand that a whole world of possibilities lies ahead of them, but Eric and Jenny would come home every night to a father who was running out of possibilities. You can't be normal under those conditions. Bob finally figured that out, and the kids were just glad for any moment that felt like old times.

"Normal" was a word Bob used to fool himself—the last of his attempts to pick the rosiest forecast. "I may not make it," he said one night to Eric and Jenny in a moment of stunning self-delusion. "*May not?*" Eric cracked. Even Bob smiled at himself.

At times his pain was so intense he would nod off, only to be snapped to consciousness by what felt like a sharp knife to the gut. Beating the cancer was no longer thinkable. In his final autumn, it was the tenderness—not the pretense that all was well—that made the inevitable bearable.

"When he got real bad, Mom and I would have to take him to the bathroom," Eric told me. "At this point he was on morphine and quite out of it. I couldn't talk to him at all on some days. Anyways, one day I got him to the toilet and he sat down. He was sitting there and I started to bite my nails. He looked up at me and it was as if all the medication drained from his system and it was Dad again. 'You've got to stop doing that, buddy,' he said. 'I know,' I said and stopped and brought him back to his bed. But for a brief moment, it was just great to have Dad back again—the guy who always called me 'buddy,' the one who was always worried about my terrible habit of biting my nails."

Sometimes Eric would just climb into bed with Bob and lie next to him, trying to remember the old times. They'd watch Yankees games together, like they always had.

"Dad and I used to always bond together during the Yankees games. Growing up, I developed this love for the team. He told me later that he wasn't a huge fan before, but of course when I became a fan, so did he. Dad would always wake me up in the mornings before school and tell me the game scores from the previous night. As I got older, I spent less time watching the games with him, but he would always give me the updates on how they were doing. That is something I miss a lot.

He always kept me updated on everything."

One night toward the end of the 1998 baseball season, Eric remembers, "I was watching the game and Dad walked out of the bedroom. The skin was kind of hanging off him. And most importantly, he was on a lot of morphine and was very confused. It was nighttime and the game was going on, but Dad thought it was morning and said, 'Eric, I missed the game last night. Did the Yankees win?' I said, 'Yeah, they're winning right now.' This really confused him. I had to sit him down and explain that his biological clock was out of whack. It took a long time, but he was extremely grateful in the end. This was tough for me because now we had switched roles. It was a pretty sad time. But Dad lightened things up. 'Why are you being so nice to me today?' he'd ask. I said: 'Dad, the Yankees are on and we always bond when the Yankees are playing.' He turned to me with a smile and said, 'Then I wish the Yankees would play every day.' I looked into his eyes and it was as if all the confusion was gone. For a split second, he didn't have cancer anymore. Thinking back on it now, it still moves me."

It was in quiet moments that Bob tried to remind Eric and Jenny that he still loved them.

It was in quiet moments that Bob tried to remind Eric and Jenny that he still loved them. It was all he had to give. The role reversal—with Eric caring for Bob and keeping him up on the Yankees games—was hard, to be sure, but beautiful at the same time. This switch of roles is a way for a loving child to help a dying parent stay connected to life in his final days. It's also a way for the parent to sense that his child will be all right, that he no longer needs the parent's physical presence. It's a way to help close the books.

It is hard to watch someone we love suffer. There were many days when I wanted to look the other way, to stay away so I wouldn't have to confront the reality of Bob's pain—pain I could do nothing about and that sometimes the drugs couldn't touch. Here is the real truth: It was pain that could be my pain someday; that is what really scared me.

That's a big part of getting close to death—seeing ourselves in the suffering of others. But just as Bob chose to keep reaching out, I chose to keep coming back to his bedside—as did so many others. I learned to approach it just as Bob approached teaching—to hang in there to see what's around the next turn.

By the final weeks, Bob was using what was left of his daily routine not to thwart the cancer but to pull himself through the day. "I know I'm dying, but I don't want to help the process along," he said one afternoon. The change was subtle, I thought, but real. He was not about to go quietly. He was going to keep as much of the life he had built as he could, for as long as he could.

As is my own routine, I was roasting corn on the cob at our parish picnic on the second Sunday in September. I've been apprenticing at the job for years and have never had any desire to advance through the ranks to become a master corn roaster. One day I may finally figure out—from the brown tone of the husk—when the corn is most succulent. It's a slow learning curve, however, and I prefer taking my time. It is one of the ways I use routine to slow the passing of years, to tell myself I have a lot of time left. I'm not ready to be in charge of the corn; I may never be. I like being the student.

As I turned the ears over the fire that afternoon, Patty called on my cell phone to tell me that Bob was so sick and in so much pain that she feared the end might be very close. It wasn't her first such call. She was flying blind. She didn't know what death would look like for Bob when it finally came. She reacted with anxiety to any change in his condition, and she wanted company at those moments.

I got to the house as soon as I could, and she had already calmed down. A bunch of McQuaid football players, including Eric, were watching a football game in the living room. Bob was in the small bedroom across from the master bedroom. He was dozing on a twin bed against one wall.

Although Bob was hardly awake and certainly not watching, a small black and white television flickered at the foot of the bed. I knew that turning it off was the quickest way to shake him back to consciousness with a request to turn it back on. For Bob, the ubiquitous TV was just another way of keeping contact, of surrounding himself with or tethering himself to action, to life. It wasn't so much a way to avoid contact with others as it was a way to avoid being alone with himself and his thoughts.

In the living room, the football players were whooping and shouting at completed passes and bone-jarring hits. Occasionally, someone would shush the crowd, remembering that Bob was resting a few feet away. Mike Pinch, one of the McQuaid players and the starting center, a senior and captain of the team, had broken his arm and was out for the year—a brutal disappointment. Since this season was Mike's last chance to stand out for McQuaid, he had hoped to use his senior year to pick up a football scholarship.

Mike had formed a special bond with Bob and wanted him to sign the cast on his arm. Mike's grandfather was diagnosed with pancreatic cancer the same week as Bob. The two of them were often at the same hospital, and Mike would visit them both after school. When Mike's grandfather died, Bob went to the funeral and promised Mike that he would do his best to beat the cancer.

When Mike was an eighth grader, he rode with Bob and Patty in a rented van on a class trip. "I found out what a great and funny guy Mr. Schwartz was on that trip," he recalls. "To tell you the truth, to this day I have no idea where we went. I don't remember anything about the trip. I just remember the ride there and back with Mr. Schwartz."

He remembered the stories and the laughs and the way Bob always made the boys know they were OK and full of promise. His students remembered how they felt around him, and they wanted to help him now that he needed them. It was in those ordinary, unscripted exchanges with students that Bob made his mark. He was genuinely interested in them—in what they thought and how they felt. And his interest made awkward teenagers feel good about themselves.

Earlier that particular Sunday morning, Mike and some of the other players had heard that Bob had died during the night. So they went to the house not knowing what to expect but wanting to be there for Eric and the Schwartz family. When they pulled up, Bob—having heard of the rumor—was sitting in a lawn chair in the front yard with a big smile on his face. He was laughing when the boys piled out of the car. Bob never missed an opportunity to laugh at death and to make people's normal apprehensions about it the butt of a joke.

The boys went in the house, relieved to be watching football instead of comforting Eric. Bob went to take a nap. As the afternoon wore on, Mike was waiting for the right moment to ask for Bob's autograph on his cast. But asking a dying man for a favor was tough for a young person who is not prepared to think about the end of life.

Finally, Mike came into the room to ask for a signature. Some of the other boys squeezed into the bedroom, while a few stood in the hall. Bob pulled himself up and gave himself another dose of morphine. The pump let out a little purring noise, and Bob stroked it. "Nice kitty," he said.

When Mike presented his arm, Bob wrote "Trade ya?" and then signed his name. As soon as the boys got a look at the inscription, they broke out laughing. The tension was gone, evaporated like dew in mid-morning sun. It was the perfect response. It meant, "Yeah, I know I'm going to die, but I don't want you to run away because of it." It meant, "You've lost a football season, but you've got your whole life ahead of you." It meant, "You can always laugh, no matter what."

It was Bob's instinctive way of reminding his young students that death is inevitable and they can't stop it, nor could they save him. But it was OK, as long as they stayed engaged in life.

Despite his death being a foregone conclusion, Bob's decline was anything but a straight line. One day he'd be spitting up blood, bent over in such pain that he could barely speak. The next day he'd pop out of bed and offer to take out the garbage. Most of the time he didn't eat or drink anything more than a few sips of water. I couldn't understand how he could be alive. How was it possible he could live without a meal (or any intravenous feeding) for more than a week in his condition? Pat Duffy just shook her head in disbelief.

I started to read some of the hospice materials written to help families and friends of dying people recognize the signs of approaching death. I wanted to know what to expect, to get some idea, based on the symptoms, how much longer Bob had. I wanted to feel I had some control—if only an ability to approximate the time of his death and brace myself accordingly.

"As eating and drinking taper off," one booklet said, "the body naturally becomes dehydrated. When this occurs, the dying person becomes sleepier and may be less aware of pain and discomfort. This is a normal part of the dying process." Bob certainly had lost interest in food, but the wind-down period was so slow that it defied prediction.

The books also advised loved ones to expect periods of apnea (not breathing) for several seconds and breathing that is alternately shallow and slow and then deeper and faster.

Other signs of impending death are restlessness or agitation, confusion, inattention, and a dulling of the senses. The fingers, earlobes and nails may take on a bluish or gray tint. The skin may be blotchy.

What was easy to miss in the literature were the warnings that approaching-death changes "are unique to every person." You could not look at the changes in Bob and know what was next, except that his death was coming. It is normal for we humans to look for certainty in mortality, but it is also futile.

With the John Denver memorial concert no longer in the cards, Bob was still determined—in his dwindling lucid moments—to make a late September trip to Nashville to the Blue Bird Café for the Songwriters' Showcase.

For days, everyone who stopped by the house was polled on the wisdom of making the trip. Bob wanted more than anything to be there, despite the fact that the stress of it would have killed him. If you have to die, why not die doing something you love, he argued. He thought there must be a way to pull it off. He told me that on many days he didn't feel any worse than he had back in August when he sang *I Gave You Each Other* in front of 5,000 people at Letchworth State Park. He just had to time his morphine correctly. But despite those moments of high energy, he was clearly worse, and weakening.

But his sister Mary bought plane tickets to Nashville for Bob and Patty and me. Initially, we thought we'd go down Friday night and spend the weekend. Bob's brother Tom, a history professor at Vanderbilt University, would put us up. But that was far too ambitious an itinerary. If it were to happen at all, we decided, it would have to be in and out.

I wanted to be there to hear him sing one last time, but I dreaded the possibility that he'd be too weak to get on stage or that he might not be able to muster enough voice to be heard. I didn't look forward to seeing him walk off the stage knowing he'd never stand in front of a microphone again. I didn't want to be there when Bob, the performer, took his last breath in front of an audience. And yet, I did want to be there *for him*. Just as Patty and Mary and all the rest of the family wanted to be there *for him*.

I felt, selfishly, that taking the trip would be good *for me*, that it would help me better understand why this one last song, in front of an audience of perfect strangers, was so important to Bob. There was nothing unusual about my feelings, but I wish I could have been more focused on what was right for Bob rather than on what would work best for me. But this death walk with a friend was uncharted territory for me, so I just did the best I could.

I am not apologizing for my feelings. Ego can be controlled, but it cannot be completely disabled. The point is that I, and all the people in Bob's life, just kept coming back. You cannot choose how you feel, you can only choose how you behave, and at least I was there for Bob.

The running debate over the Nashville road trip continued, even as Bob's funeral planning began. Family photos were spread across the dining room table and the sidebar conversations centered on the best ones to display during the wake. He'd be buried from Holy Family Church, where he was baptized and received his First Communion and Confirmation. Pallbearers were selected; the music was planned, as was the post-funeral meal.

It's not uncommon to plan one's own funeral. It is a way of winding down, of saying good-bye and reconciling oneself to the end of this phase of life. It's also a way to take control of death, rather than being controlled by it. In an odd way, picking out songs and readings and assigning various roles to family and friends is a way to tame death— much, I suppose, as paratroopers might joke with each other before leaping into the black, hoping to control the moment, knowing that soon their lives will be up to fate.

But for Bob, funeral planning "ultimately became conflicted," Father Jim Schwartz explains. "He wanted the funeral his way. He controlled every detail. He wanted it to mean something to people, but he didn't want to talk about it—about its meaning. Because, again, that would involve letting go. It was the last jump he couldn't take."

John and Joe Dady, Irish singers from Rochester and friends of Bob's, agreed to do the music. Joe worried about one of the songs Bob wanted: a traditional Irish tune called *Isn't It Grand?* The chorus gives you the drift of it—"Let's not have a sniffle, let's have a bloody good cry. And always remember—the longer you live, the sooner you'll bloody well die." But it was Bob's call. They'd sing it if that's what he wanted.

After an hour or so of funeral planning one evening, the conversation looped around to the idea of "killing time."

"That's such an awful expression," Bob said weakly. "As if time weren't worth very much. I don't want to kill time; I want to enjoy it."

"We all talk about 'the grind,'" Bob said, "but there has to be more than the crush of the grind if people are going to be happy. I know people can't always get jobs they like, but there's something wrong with going to the same job year after year and hating it. Just look at how we let jobs kill us—'I was lost in a merger. It hurts, but not that much.'"

"You are lucky," I said, realizing immediately that I could have found a better choice of words. "You had a job you loved. You always had the music. So you didn't have to 'kill time.'"

Bob agreed, and I said that I'm the same way: "I've got a job I love; it took me almost thirty years, but finally I've got my own soapbox and get paid to use it. What could be better?"

It's funny, we agreed, that people who hate their jobs revile people who have jobs they like—as if no one should be happy working, as if you're not earning your pay if you do something you enjoy.

Finally, Bob quipped, "We've killed enough time for one day." He and I hugged each other, and I went home.

Word of the funeral-planning spread, and people wanted to stop in for final good-byes to Bob. But the last thing Bob wanted was people crying on his shoulder. Not that anyone knew it then, but he still had two months to live.

He rallied one last time. On a Saturday afternoon, John Dady came for a visit, bringing his nine-year-old daughter Mara, a precocious red-head who hit it off with Bob every time they met.

Somehow, at the sight of Mara, the morphine grogginess disappeared. Bob literally jumped out of bed, grabbed his guitar, and marched out to the front lawn, where he played tunes with John Dady and Paul Swiatek. Bob hadn't had the strength to pick up the guitar in weeks.

"It was supposed to be Bob's last weekend alive," Swiatek says, recalling the urgent word that had traveled around Bob's circle of friends. "I had to chuckle at it as I drove home. What happened was we went from the extraordinary (Bob's lying in bed, filled with cancer) to the ordinary (playing guitar on the lawn). That's what we always did when were together at Bob's house."

That day for me, however, was the start of a complicated but moving spiritual odyssey that would not end with Bob's death. Bob's friends would lift him toward God, giving him a welcome taste of the life he was soon to have, and reminding him that he was not alone. All of us— the Communion of Saints—were taking a communal journey to God, and Bob was just a little ahead of the rest of us.

What Catholics believe is that the living and the dead help each other along the road that is full of hazards and blind turns. It is a deeply comforting belief—the knowledge that we are all walking the same path and that others have walked this path before us—that they are waiting on the other side, praying to God for the grace we will need.

Those last two months, Bob's friends walked the path with him, not knowing when it would end, not knowing just what we could do for him, but hoping our presence would make his dying less frightening. Even more important, we wanted to make Bob's death an affirmation of his life and all he cared about.

After Bob died, I got a letter from an acquaintance of his who happened to visit that Saturday afternoon and described what he saw.

Over the years, the man wrote, he had known Bob as a performer who "could play too long, ramble with stories in-between songs, and have you wondering if you were laughing with him or at him."

But on this day, he said, "Bob was curled into insignificance. I thought of E.T., crumpled in a field, dying because he couldn't get home. His eyes began to roll in his head...always a Bob trait, that flutter of lashes and the lolling eyeball losing focus, as if turning sight inward for the true illumined response."

His voice that day was clear and strong, nothing nasally or off-key about it.

Bob's voice was "thin and cracking, his head too heavy to raise...beseeching another dose of morphine to tube up his side. I thought I might be viewing a man whose breath could stop in the next second—a living corpse late for the grave."

But, the letter continued, "Music spilled in from the living room." And Bob struggled to get up and play. He told Patty that he'd be out after he took a little nap.

For an hour or more, people wandered in and out of the room. Bob dozed but was not responsive until Mara arrived. "A girl...with the dew of Ireland in her skin," is how the letter described her. "Her innocence drew Bob's head from the pillow, his back uprighted to a sitting position. 'Well, if you've come to see me, I've got to get up,' he said. 'But only if you'll sing a song with me.' Mara didn't respond. Out came Bob's bare legs from beneath their covers. The man curled in his bed like an infant was now standing, his voice even."

Bob got dressed—in a nightshirt—and went to the lawn. "His voice that day was clear and strong, nothing nasally or off-key about it." They played *Sloop John B* and *Both Sides Now* and Bob Dylan's *Forever Young*.

The traffic moved along as always, a lawn mower rumbled nearby, and the friend heard Bob as never before that day: "Someone bold enough to be laughed at, undaunted by the pitfalls of pitch and expectation, accepting and able to expose—in its beauty and imperfection—his soul. It stood there, bursting forth from all the countable ribs, the sunken shoulders, the iridescent eyes. It had always been that way. I think Bob just wanted us to listen."

I often think of that afternoon as Bob's Transfiguration. The story reminds me of the time Jesus took some of his apostles up a mountain and there appeared with Abraham and Moses, all in white, radiant in the brilliant light of heaven. It was a moment for the apostles to step back and consider the reward that would one day be theirs—if they would but be faithful.

There on the Schwartz front lawn, Bob—the same Bob whose senses had been dulled for weeks by morphine—was suddenly *transformed* by a child's innocent laughter, by his memories of the old days, by his music. It was as if time stood still, as if he was never sick at all. It was a reminder of what once was. And of the happiness he would have again, even if not in this world.

They played about forty-five minutes. And then, as suddenly as he had jumped out of bed, Bob got up and went inside. He never played the guitar again.

A couple of days later, Bob had to make his decision about Nashville. Time was running out. Early one evening just a few days shy of the Songwriters' Showcase, a bunch of us were sitting in the living room. "Should I go or not?" Bob asked. "I want everyone's opinion. No taking a pass. Should I go to Nashville?"

What I remember is the silence. No one wanted to answer. Our job was to help him, but no one wanted to preempt the few choices he had left in his life. Finally, someone asked, "What do *you* want, Bob?"

"I want to go," he said. "I think I'd be all right. But Dr. Garrow says it's too risky."

Patty finally said she didn't want to lose him like that, just to sing one song. Someone else suggested that—through Bob's many McQuaid connections—it might be possible to get a company jet to shuttle him down and back in one day. If he could get on the plane Sunday afternoon, fly to Nashville, and hop right back when he finished at the Bluebird, he wouldn't have the stress of a whole weekend away.

I finally said that I thought Bob should do what he wanted to do, that it was his life and his call.

Today I recognize it is one thing to say over a few beers that it's better to die doing something you love than to be careful and buy a little more time, but it's quite another thing to encourage someone else to "go for it" when cancer is closing in and the days are short.

I know it was Bob's decision to make, but still I feel I chickened out that evening. I wish I had been more attuned to reality of Bob's struggle to move from this life to the next. It was my job—*our* job—to help him make that jump, to help him realize he didn't have anything left to prove. I should have told him I loved him, lots of people loved him, and the way he'd always lived his life was proof positive that he was no quitter. One more trip wouldn't add a thing to the legacy. My words probably wouldn't have changed anything. But at that moment, I had no insight. I didn't know what to do or say.

We reached no consensus on the trip, but I knew he wouldn't make it. Bob had wanted a resounding vote of support, and he didn't get it. I think, too, he realized from the Saturday concert on the lawn that he could no longer predict when or if he could play at all. It was not just a question of timing the morphine dose, as it had been during the summer. As he had said many times before, "Cancer dictates; I am just the stenographer."

The conversation shifted direction. Patty and Bob began to recall Halloweens past, and all the kids who paraded through their neighborhood in bright costumes. In recent years, the numbers had thinned out, and a few miniature Snickers bars were enough for the traffic.

"This year," Bob vowed. "I'll be the trick-or-treater with orange on his face. That's how you'll know I'm still here."

"Don't even talk about coming back to haunt me," Patty said. We all laughed, knowing that if he could Bob would—just for a hoot. It was one of those transitioning-to-death conversations, half serious, half playful, that helped the two of them imagine the world as it soon would be.

People started to leave, and Bob went for a shave. I went to keep him company and to make sure his hand was still steady enough to wield a blade. He reminisced about friends whose marriages have come apart. "I always ask, 'Have you told your wife you love her recently?' They always say, 'No.'"

Suddenly, he wondered about heaven—another transitioning-to-death chat. He said he'd seen visions of his mother as a younger woman, and "she was so beautiful. When I get to heaven, will I see her at that age, or as she was when she died? What about John Denver—will he look like he did in Houston in 1997, a little overweight and drunk? Or will he look like he did in 1972? Younger and thinner and happier?"

When you're in heaven, I said, you're at your best—whenever that was. That's how you'll be. I had never thought whether that meant young or old—just that you'd spend eternity as an improved version of the best person you had become. "You, Bob, will be as you were all those years at McQuaid—at your peak," I said. And I thought to myself: "Casting fire on the earth, molding minds, building men"—as he sings in *Half a Hundred Years*. That was his best; that's how God will preserve him forever.

The Nashville trip never came up again. Whatever disappointment Bob had, he kept to himself. And I was glad he didn't put me on the spot again.

His hour drew near. The Communion of Saints had gathered. In a way only understood through faith, Bob's dying was drawing all of us closer to God. His dying reminded us how much we depend on each other—and this is exactly as God intended.

A Bloody Good Cry

About a week after the Nashville trip-that-wasn't, it was obvious that not going was the right decision. Bob Schwartz's voice was barely a whisper. His idea of a meal was a gummy worm and a half a piece of bread with margarine. The traffic was still heavy through the living room, but Bob slept through most of it.

The ordeal was exhausting for Patty, but it made her stronger and better, just as it did Bob. "We definitely became a lot closer when Bob got sick," she says. Before then, they had their share of troubles. A marriage counselor once told them he had never seen a couple less suited to each other. But they stuck with their marriage because they loved each other. We often think love is an emotion—but it's really a promise, a conscious, deliberate act.

People who love each other put the other first. That's what they promise when they stand before God and vow to be true in sickness and in health, "till death do you part." In sickness, Bob and Patty came as close as they ever had to the ideal Bob described in his song, *For My Wife*, written before he ever met Patty:

> To shine for me in morning, when there is no light
> To bring around the evening, when there is no night

This is all I ask of you, my dear
This is all I ask of you

To let me walk you anywhere that you might want to go
And to let me tell you anything that you may want to know

To let me kiss away the tear that I have caused to fall
And to make you smile till you forget it had to fall at all

Now, as his days grew fewer, Bob needed Patty to shine for him when he had no more light—even as he tried to make up for any tears he had caused her that he hadn't kissed away before.

From the moment his cancer was diagnosed, Patty decided her job was Bob. At first, that meant getting him to treatments, sharing his determination to beat the cancer, communicating with the vast Schwartz network, and making sure that Bob was accessible to everyone. In the final weeks, her job was to gently prepare him for the inevitable. She used the funeral planning to let Bob know that she knew. They picked a cemetery and a funeral director; they talked about insurance and Eric's transition to college. By October, her job was to help him die, without ever saying it in so many words. Her job was to help him understand that it was OK to let go.

Patty never forced hospice on Bob against his will. She and the kids certainly tired of Bob's dying. They felt the weight of his care. They longed for relief. But they *did* the right thing—even when they didn't feel they could take any more. They stayed right there for him.

One night as I got up to leave, Patty gave me a hug and whispered that she had told Pat the nurse she was going to start limiting the visits so she and the kids could have a little quality time alone with Bob. Pat Duffy was direct: "You've already had your quality time."

It was true, of course. But the starkness of the reality hit hard. Patty had been waiting for *their* time with Bob, and it had slipped away. I told her not to worry about everybody else. If she thought it was best to tell visitors to stay away for a while, then that was right thing to do. "Just trust your instincts," I said.

Dying brings a sense of urgency. The dying person sees so much left undone and tries to step up the pace of life, even as life is slipping away. Loved ones suddenly realize that the time to say things long left unsaid is disappearing. The trouble is we often don't know what to say or how to say it. I remember when my own father was dying, worn down from emphysema, I wished we could talk about important things—about what he was feeling and fearing, about his favorite memories. But I didn't know how to begin such a conversation, and neither did he. At a moment when time requires us to be simple and direct, we stammer and backfill the conversation with observations on the weather, the change of seasons, the consistency of the pasta sauce, or last night's late Yankees' score.

But we learn about death, as we learn about life—through trial and error. Over time, we become more familiar (though not necessarily more comfortable) with the vagaries of dying. The second or third time we go through the dying experience with a loved one, some of us learn to get past the shock. We marvel at the way life becomes so much more vital as death becomes more real. We discover that helping a dying person move toward God makes our own lives richer.

Bob's deathbed was his last classroom. It was a demonstration that while good health is surely a blessing, what matters in life is how we have *mattered*.

During one of my lunchtime visits near the very end, I sat next to Bob while he dozed, so Patty could step outside for a cigarette. Bob looked smaller every day. His kneecaps and pelvic bones formed unnaturally sharp ridges. His wrists were so thin I think I could have circled them with my thumb and index finger. His face was sunken, his hair dry, even brittle. His breathing was shallow and labored. His eyelids would occasionally spring open like window shades, but there was nothing in his eyes. He would stare at the ceiling; his gaze no longer flickering with hope or humor or anything at all.

I watched him for a few minutes, then let my mind wander between *The Price Is Right*—playing on Bob's ubiquitous TV—and the heavy October raindrops slapping against the windowpanes. After thirty minutes or so, Bob woke up. He was back again, but not for long.

"What are you thinking?" I asked.

"I'm losing time," he said. "I never know what time it is. I'm always asking. I never had to do that before. I really want to know what time it is." He was almost pleading for time. "It's a few minutes after one o'clock," I said, not realizing at first that was not what he wanted to know.

He wanted to know how much time he had left. Of course he did. By that time I was getting comfortable being present to his dying, but I had no idea how to answer such a question. I tried. I said something like "as much time as you'll need, Bob. That's how much you'll have." But even as I said it, I knew it probably didn't make any sense to him. It didn't even make sense to me.

This, I realized later, is why it's so important for all of us to be there for each other. Bob was being laid low by cancer, forced to replay his life in his mind, worried that he had failed, wondering if he'd be remembered. But we were all part of the bridge that would eventually take him to eternal peace. He wanted the quiet reassurance of his friends and family. He needed to hear again and again that he had lived well, that he had mattered. It was our job to let him know he had, and I think all of us succeeded. In the end, Bob's was a good death, even if he fought it with every ounce of life he had.

All of Bob's final days were filled with pain and, sometimes, confusion. His visions continued, as they often do when someone nears death, but they were less disturbing to Bob as time wore on. A month before he died he began seeing the Virgin Mary. Sometimes she was in the kitchen. He could see her peeling bananas one day and yelled at Patty that it was rude to let the Mother of God do kitchen work. Bob's deceased Uncle Nick usually appeared in the bedroom. Bob's mother, May, visited him regularly as well.

On occasion, it was possible to get Bob to talk about the afterlife. In moments of intense pain, he did sometimes despair. When the pain was so bad he thought he was about to die, he wondered if there is a God. But when the pain eased, so did his doubts.

The wavering is normal, even inevitable. Bob had been raised in the bosom of the Church. In high school, he had wanted to be a priest, and when that dream faded he had committed himself to a career teaching in Catholic education—which one pursues for love, not money. Everyone who knew Bob knew him as a man of great faith, and yet amidst his dying he spoke of faith only in passing. In fact, I wondered more than once if Bob's faith had failed him when he needed it most. But now I believe that Bob's faith led him to hold on to life, not to surrender it.

Not long before Bob died, Tony Trama, another teacher at McQuaid, asked him if he believed in God: "Do you *really believe*? Is there another place out there?" Bob was all loaded up with morphine, Tony says, "but he had this frightened look on his face, like he just did not know any more."

That look was oddly comforting to Tony, even as it was distressing. "I thought—not right away but later—that this is good. Even Bob, as good as he was, was afraid. Just like any of us would be."

Faith is easiest when we need it least—when all is well. But it is when all is not well that we need faith. In that circumstance, our grip on faith tightens and then loosens. It is not constant. It is always there, but it is not always easy to express. Bob told his students not to blame God for his death, but I'm sure he felt his own prayer for a cure was not answered. I'm sure he was angry with God, as Job was. He didn't like the plan God seemed to have for him.

Bob still believed, but he would not accept his fate, even as his series of small victories turned into small defeats. One afternoon I found him in the bathroom shaving with the electric razor the oncology nurses had given him weeks earlier—when they believed he no longer had the steady hand he needed to wield a blade. It seemed so ordinary, almost a non-event. But it was a metaphor for the end that was now stalking him, waiting for its chance to bring him down: He had used a razor blade for the last time; Aspen and Nashville didn't happen; he was on more drugs than ever; he couldn't eat; he couldn't play the guitar.

But even as he was aware that he was losing to cancer, he did everything he could to push it back.

Pat Duffy, the hospice nurse, said she had never seen a clearer case of death denial, and I am sure she was right. I had not thought of it that way, because Bob always acknowledged that cancer was wearing him down and always joked about dying. But even as he was aware that he was losing to cancer, he did everything he could to push it back. This was the man who recognized early in the course of his cancer that he was trying to plan for "no future." That's why he turned his attention to the present. Denial worked for Bob—if the idea of living is to fight to stay alive.

He was like a hitter who can no longer get around on a ninety-six-mile-per-hour fastball. He just tries to foul off pitch after pitch. Maybe he'll get a walk. Maybe the pitcher will throw him something a little slower that he can drive. The hitter knows he's overmatched, but he doesn't stand there with a bat on his shoulder waiting for the umpire to call him out.

There were, of course, those in-between moments when Bob was thinking out loud about death yet reaching back to the wit that had served him so well in life. "I didn't talk with Bob about his impending death, because I don't think he wanted to admit that death was not going away," his brother Joe recalls, "but two months before he died I was visiting and holding his hand as he lay in bed. I started to cry and told him how much I was going to miss him. Without opening his eyes, Bob got very serious and said, 'When you hear the leaves in the trees rustling, I'll be there.' He paused for a moment and then said, 'When you look at the discount bin in the music store, I'll be there too.' I couldn't help but laugh. I looked up to see the smile on his face."

Bob also freely shared one of his final visions with anyone who'd listen: "I have a dream that I'm in heaven and John Denver is there, and he says, 'Hi, Bob, wanna take a ride in my plane?'"

At the start of his final month, his body filled with cancer, Bob wanted to try chemo one more time. He hadn't wanted to quit the chemo when Dr. Garrow took him off of it, and now he wanted to try it again. All of us, including Bob I am sure, knew it was futile, but straws were all he had left to grasp.

Personally, I think Bob would have found the peace he wanted sooner than he did if he had allowed himself some quiet time for reflection—if he had limited the traffic through the bedroom, in effect. But that was not Bob's way of doing things. The commotion made it easy never to be alone with his thoughts. It enabled, if you will, his denial. I don't offer that as a criticism. That's just how Bob Schwartz was, right up until the end. He showed me that we, the Communion of Saints, are pilgrims who make it through the desert because we have each other. Bob just took that thought to the nth degree.

For most of us, I think, it is certainly helpful—in a spiritually cleansing kind of way—to be able to pull back, to escape into one's thoughts and prayers, especially when we are coming to the end of our days. That part of it just didn't work for Bob.

He was trapped on a course he didn't choose, and he fought it all the way. Death would pull him down, and he would look for all the world like a corpse, lying rigid and cold on the bed, slack jawed, eyes glassy and fixed. And then life would take a turn with him. He'd have a great time watching the movie *Animal House* for the hundredth time, or listening to the complete works of Bob Dylan for the thousandth time.

Laughter was so much a part of Bob that, for him, humor was the last sense to go. One night Patty got up with him when he said he was about to have a bowel movement. "What was I thinking?" she said the next morning. "He hadn't eaten anything in days." Anyway, Bob was sitting on the toilet for twenty minutes or so. When she came back for him, he looked up at her and said, "Does this mean I'm going to have to pee like a woman now?"

"Bob's humor helped soften the blow for the people he loved," says his brother Joe. "When I visited Bob, he wanted to sit up in a chair and visit like a regular person, but he could barely speak. We were sitting around talking and the name Schwartz came into the conversation. Bob had an old line—'Schwartz was German for Stop Thief.' I looked at Bob and a small but visible smile came through. It was heartbreaking to think his personality and love of life was trapped inside."

Bob didn't know how to handle people who wanted to tell him how sorry they were and how much they'd miss him. His humor often smoothed the wrinkles out of what would otherwise have been bumpy conversations, but it also stopped Bob from mourning himself.

That's how it was in Bob's deathbed classroom. Everyone who set foot inside could say it would be easier if he'd just do this, or it was harder than it should have been because he wouldn't try that. And all of those observations may have been perfectly valid, but the point was that Bob could only be Bob and it was up to us to help him (as he was, not as we might have wished him to be) to return to God.

Bob wasn't trying to make his death easier. He wanted to live, so he just kept living. A "peaceful" death is not an entitlement, nor is it necessary for salvation. Bob's death was holy, it was honest, it was the way he wanted it to be.

On Monday November 2, the start of Bob's final fortnight, I sat next to his bed in his room at the house for fifteen minutes and prayed a rosary—something I had not done in years. The sun was bright in the window, and outside this tiny room life was as it always is. Yet it all seemed very far away. All I could see was Bob.

At least three times he stopped breathing, but each time he came back. I was tiring of this wake. I hated to see Patty so exhausted that she couldn't eat or sleep. She was almost afraid to take a shower for fear he'd die without her. She knew how much he needed her. Even when he couldn't talk, which was most of the time now, he seemed to appreciate her presence. She took comfort in that.

Patty was his final link to the life he struggled so mightily to keep. As death neared, they became the couple he wrote about years earlier in *Take and Wear This Ring*.

> *I'm never far from you*
> *In all we say and do*
> *And should we be apart*
> *You are ever in my heart.*
>
> Chorus:
>
> *Take and wear this ring*
> *As a sign of love*
> *Let me hear you sing*
> *You are mine, my love*
> *In sickness and in health*
> *In poverty and in wealth*
> *Through the joy and through the pain*
> *In sunshine and in rain.*

It is funny how you become your words. Often a writer's words reflect the ideals he holds precious and hopes to live long enough to attain. Certainly that was so with Bob. And just as cancer had made Bob and Patty better individuals, it made them better spouses. Like so many couples, they often found it easier to be good to others than to each other. But in crisis, their commitment held them together.

When I finished my rosary, I went into the living room. Patty asked Pat Duffy, "So, another weekend?"

"I don't think so," she said.

"I hope not," I thought to myself. And then I had those thoughts again: I was angry that Bob wouldn't let go, that he left his wife and family and friends waiting—almost wishing—for him to die. And I knew that when he died I'd feel guilty for these thoughts. I told myself I'd never allow myself to hang on this way. How foolish of me. I should have learned over all those months that dying isn't a multiple-choice quiz. You don't pick your death, or its time, or even the way you die. Bob was dying the only way he could, and so will we all.

The next afternoon, Pat Duffy said very matter-of-factly that this was likely Bob's last night. His blood pressure was way down. He was sleeping hard and his breathing continued to be very uneven. Patty had spent most of the morning cleaning the house, perhaps anticipating that it would soon be full of mourners.

I went into the bedroom where Bob slept. I whispered an Our Father and a Hail Mary close to his ear. I sat down and wondered about the message from God for me in all of this. I heard no voice from afar, no whisper in the quiet valleys of my mind. But I wished that I could always appreciate life the way Bob did. I kissed him on the forehead and started to leave. I had heard so often that he was about die that I didn't take Pat Duffy's prediction to heart. Indeed, she was wrong.

A couple of days later, Patty asked several friends to stop in to speak the words Bob never wanted to hear—good-bye.

We were supposed to tell him that it's all right to let go, that he doesn't have to hold on for anyone else's sake. Pat Duffy said we should give him permission to go home to God. This permission to die is a common hospice practice. Dying people often need to know that the people they love are ready to let go and that their debts and obligations have been settled and forgiven.

It was, however, new to me. I was very anxious. I wasn't sure how to say good-bye. I could only hope the words would come when I stood there over his bed. They were not coming as I drove to the house. I wasn't sure it was even the right thing to do. Obviously something was playing out in Bob's mind. I wondered if we should just let his death happen whenever it was going to.

I wanted to do right by him. Finally, though, I trusted Patty and Pat Duffy.

At Bob's bedside were Patty, Vicki Bida and Tony Gross. "Bob, it's OK to die," Vicki was saying. She held his hand and leaned close to his face. He seemed to nod slightly in agreement. Months earlier, she told me, she had tried to talk to him about his death. "He stood up and yelled, 'Don't say that; don't *ever* say that!'" But on this afternoon, she was saying it again, hoping to let him turn the page to a new chapter.

Tony said similar gentle words and kissed him on the cheek. A mother of one of the McQuaid hockey players just happened to stop by. She was carrying a letter from her son. But she couldn't read it without crying. Vicki took it from her and read the note to Bob. It was a lovely tribute. The young man described Bob as the person who had most influenced the course of his life. If Bob still was looking for proof that he had mattered, he had yet another piece of evidence.

Everyone but me left the room. I promised Bob that I would handle this book and tell his story. I told him that I felt honored to have been invited into his life and that he had been my teacher too. I had learned from him how important it is to be true to my values, to myself, and to each moment.

I pulled a prayer card out of my wallet. A priest I hadn't talked to in years had sent it to me. It had arrived in that morning's mail. It was St. Francis' peace prayer, and I read it for Bob.

The words repeatedly stuck in my throat. I was nervous. I could feel tears spilling from the corners of both eyes. I read:

> Lord, make me an instrument of your peace.
> Where there is hatred, let me sow love;
>   where there is injury, pardon;
>   where there is doubt, faith;
>   where there is despair, hope;
>   where there is darkness, light;
>   where there is sadness, joy.
>
> Grant that I may not so much seek
>   to be consoled as to console;
> to be understood as to understand;
>   to be loved as to love.
>
> For it is in giving that we receive;
> it is in pardoning that we are pardoned;
> and it is in dying that we are born to eternal life.

"You've done all of this, Bob," I said. "Your work is finished. Rest."

He had drifted off to sleep again. I joined the others in the living room. But a short while later, Tony and I went back in; Bob was awake.

Tony kissed him again. "I love you," he said.

"Me, too, Bob," I said. "It's OK. Jesus is waiting for you." I kissed him again.

"I gotta go," he said ever so softly. "But I can't." He squeezed my hand with what little strength he had left. "Get some sleep," I said. "I love you. We all love you." I choked out the words. I knew the long watch was almost over. I felt a sense of impending loss. I didn't want to let him go. I wanted to help him in some basic way, but I didn't know what to do. Again, I just sat there. Sadness, like a cold rain, left me shaking and empty. Patience, as always, was necessary, but I was tired of myself and my wildly swinging feelings.

I have thought about that moment many times since. I have told many people over and over: Just be there; you cannot stop death; you cannot resolve a dying person's inner conflicts. But it is not enough. I felt helpless, and I hate that feeling more than any other.

Almost three years after Bob died, I attended a Lenten retreat where Sister Mary Lou Mitchell, a sister of St. Joseph with a Ph.D. in nursing, spoke. Right at the start of her talk she said, "Cancer people are the healthiest people I know." Her twin sister had breast cancer, and Sister Mary Lou spent a lot of time with her at the hospital. She was amazed at her spirit: "I realized that I could never say again that health is a physical condition."

I went to see her later to ask her to continue that thought. "There are as many ways to die as there are people," she said. "We think there is a right way. We think we can control it. If we're ready to die, then we'll just die. But it's not so. You could be as ready as anyone ever has been, and then hang on for days."

Why, I wondered, would someone—especially someone with deep faith—want to hang on when there is no hope for survival? "Death is a mystery," she said. "How do you get in touch with a mystery?" There is so much going on inside the dying person, we can only hope to glimpse it, not fully understand it.

Sister Mary Lou suggested I read a chapter in a book called *The Con-*

templative Heart by James Finley, who has written about the works of Thomas Merton, the Trappist monk and philosopher. The chapter was titled "The Divinity of What Just Is."

Read Finley's words slowly. Speak them aloud and let them seep quietly into your consciousness: "We ask, 'How is it possible to live a contemplative way of life in the midst of today's world? In response we are invited back into the intimate domain of our own experience of traveling along a path of everyday life in which everything appears to be nothing more that it appears to be, when suddenly, without warning, the ground beneath our feet is Mystery. The gossamer veil of appearance dissolves in an ever so subtle, ever so overwhelming realization that the present moment is unexplainably more than it appears to be. Without warning, we find ourselves falling into the abyss of a star-strewn sky or find our heart impaled by a child's laughter or the unexpected appearance of the beloved's face. Without warning, we lose our footing in the silence broken and, in the breaking deepened, by the splash of a frog we did not know was there…. God in his eternal stillness is hidden from every mortal eye. God in her eternal dancing is manifested everywhere."

At the time, I surely did not see Bob's measured march to death as just "what is." I was sure there was a reason for every step.

If Bob didn't know how not to fight, I didn't know how to accept what was happening. He was drifting; no one was in control. Nobody could either stop him from dying or help him to die.

So we—his friends, his fellow jumpers, his Communion of Saints—kept trying to move him along. I was never sure of my own motives. Did I just want him to be in that better place, or was it that I didn't want to watch anymore, that I was tired of the ride and wanted to get back to normal? Bob's deathbed classroom did not provide all the answers. The teacher didn't have them, and the students were left trying to figure them out.

A day before Patty decided she had to move Bob to hospice, she, Pat Duffy and I stood around his bed telling him that the bridge was clear, that he could cross. His Mom was there, we said, so were John Denver and Steve Goodman. The kids would be fine; there are no more loose ends to tie up.

When we were finished, as only he could, Bob said softly, "I guess I don't get a vote here. It's OK. I agree with everything you are saying." Those were the last words I heard him speak. But agreeing with what he heard didn't make it any easier to cross that bridge. He had chosen to fight for all the time he could get. It was the perfectly natural extension of all the choices he'd made over the years—choices to enjoy life and to taste its fullness with and through the people he knew and loved. It was a good choice. It made letting go harder than it might have been for someone else. But there was nothing wrong with that—except that it collided with our expectation of what a "good" death looked like.

On and off that night, Bob popped out of bed. He had literally forgotten how to walk. He had to be helped to put one foot in front of the other. Alone in the middle of the night, he fell flat on his back. He fell hard. Nothing was broken, but Patty could not let him continue to wander.

Late the next morning, the ambulance came to take him to St. Mary's Hospice. The hospice, a wonderfully caring and homelike setting, was in the former St. Mary's Hospital—where Bob and all his siblings had been born. It was just a few blocks from the Colvin Street home where he grew up. Still, I have no doubt that had he been fully aware that he was going to hospice he would have fought it all the way.

His brother John was in the living room with his wife Carol and sister Mary. Father Jim Fisher, president of McQuaid was there, as were a few other friends.

All I remember about those minutes waiting for the ambulance was Bob's frozen smile. His face was bony. He could barely pull his lips apart. His eyes were wide open, and he looked confused about what was happening to him. At last the ambulance came, and he was gone, never to return to the home he had made with Patty, Eric and Jenny.

John was stunned at how fast the hospital bed was dismantled. "It was as if Patty was in a hurry to get life back to normal. It was just so fast."

It may have seemed that way, but Bob's death was so long and so slow that Patty needed things to anchor *her*, to remind her that there was still such a thing as "normal life." Getting her bedroom back was a reminder. That was both good and bad.

She knew Bob's death was very close, but like everyone else—*more so* than everyone else—she knew that "normal" would mean life without Bob. And though she was as solid as a rock throughout Bob's long ordeal, she was on the cusp of collapse—physical, emotional and spiritual.

When I arrived at St. Mary's the next day at noontime, Bob was in the visitor's lounge, seated in an overstuffed chair. A television played in the background. Bob was still agitated. He wouldn't sit still and soon he was standing. Patty was steadying him. That's when I noticed Bob's younger brother Tom, the Vanderbilt professor, who had just arrived from Nashville.

He was standing a few feet behind Bob, his arms sort of wrapped around himself. I could see he was shocked and trying to keep himself together. He hadn't seen Bob for several weeks—back when it was still possible to have a simple conversation with him. Now Bob was rigid, unable to bend his arms or legs. His skin was cold and ashen. His eyes were wide open but unfocused.

Tom hugged his brother. Grief washed over him. He shook as he tried to stretch out that last hug.

After a few minutes, I asked Tom to come with me to the cafeteria and get a bite of lunch. As we stood in the line, moving our trays slowly past the Jell-O salads, the rolls and butter pats, Tom said that Bob "was always the George Bailey of our family"—a reference to the Jimmy Stewart character in *It's a Wonderful Life*. "He always talked of going to California or New York or Nashville, but he never did." Four of the seven Schwartz children—Mary, Tom, Rose and Gerianne—had moved away from Rochester. Bob was the one who had the wanderlust the worst, but he was, finally, drawn even more intensely to his roots, his family, and his students.

Bob would have loved to have been famous, but he wanted to be the rock more than he wanted to be a rock star. He wanted to be the guy who was always there, the guy you could count on. He made his choice—and yet he found a way to stay connected to the world of music too.

And like George Bailey, he had a chance to see what his world might have been like without him. Not through the eyes of a guardian angel, but in the eyes of students and friends and family who stayed with him. If ever a man had a chance to find out how much he meant to so many people, it was Bob Schwartz.

Even in his last two days, he was agitated. A nurse restrained him, tying his wrists to the side rails so he couldn't pull himself out and fall. As I sat with him, I wrote in my notebook, "In his bed, he looks so small and old." Bob was disappearing before my eyes.

You read all the time about people wanting to die with dignity—to take charge of their final days or moments, to direct the way they slip into the arms of God before death becomes too ugly.

Not Bob. He was almost back to the beginning of life: helpless in his bed, tied down, diapered, nearly naked, his face locked into a grimace.

George Garrow doesn't believe Bob was in physical pain during those last days. "At least I have to tell myself that," the doctor says. "We had given him everything possible."

"He was in what we call terminal anguish," says Debbie Sigrist, one of Bob's hospice nurses. "He was wrestling with the angel of death right to the end." Most of the time, people wind down and give in to the inevitable. "Dying is like giving birth; the more you yield to it, the easier it is to be taken away. If you grip the railing and tighten up, it's very hard."

From the nurses' perspective, Debbie says, "Patients like Bob are the most frustrating. There is nothing we can do to comfort them. It is important to get the pain under control so that the dying person can settle down and get ready. Terminal anguish is different. It breaks right through any restful state." She points out that people display an intensity and determination that seems impossible when the body is so weak.

As Debbie sees it, "People cannot control their thoughts, especially when they are so medicated. To those of us watching, it looks horrible, but we don't know what's going on inside the dying person's mind." Perhaps, wrestling with the angel of death is necessary, she says, a way to sort through the final unresolved conflicts in a person's life. We just don't know. It is a mystery. There are as many ways to die as there are people.

"Bob didn't fail Dying 101," she says. "He just was who he was."

The anguish of the loved one is at least partially an expression of the chasm between what we are seeing and what we expected to see—the "good death," orderly and restful, versus the reality of fear, panic, and a struggle to hold onto faith.

It was very hard for me to accept the holiness of Bob's death at first. Here was a man who had lived a virtuous life. He was faithful to his principles and to his faith. In dying, he surrounded himself with friends, as he had in life. He always drew strength from his people. Watching him die, it was easy to be discouraged. Not even his friends and family seemed able to settle him, to finally allow him to achieve peace.

But who is to say he should have found peace weeks or even days before he did? It's true that some people who are more prone than Bob to inner reflection do find acceptance of death sooner than he did. And those people, because of their pacific demeanor, in many ways become the role models for the rest of us.

Bob's was a different kind of role model. He was the energizer, always finding the best in others, encouraging them to know themselves and to be light for others. He knew instinctively that most people need the reassurance of others to have the confidence to act. He knew that because that's what he needed himself, right to the end. This idea that the right way to die is to suck it up, retreat into oneself, and ask nothing of the people around us is not for everyone, just as it was not for Bob.

What matters is not *how* we go to God, but *that* we get to God. Most of us will need help staying on course. Again, faith is essential. Bob lived well. There was no reason to doubt that he would—at a moment we could not anticipate—find eternal peace. We need faith, not to validate what we see, but to trust God even when we cannot divine the divine plan. Of course, this is easier said than done.

On the day before he died, people were coming and going, as always in Bob's life. George Garrow came and stood at Bob's side, holding his hand for several minutes. There was nothing more George could do for Bob. He was there as a friend, not a doctor.

That Saturday was a horrible day. The whole time I was there, Bob groaned and grimaced, tears seeped out of both eyes. I prayed for his death, even if he did not.

The next day, the last day, I again came by in the afternoon. The nurses had upped the concentration of Dilaudid. It seemed to have calmed him down.

As I was arriving, Paul Swiatek was leaving. He had just finished serenading his old teacher and friend. "We were just doing what we always did—playing the music," he says. He remembers playing a song called *Across the Great Divide* by Kate Wolf. It's a lovely ballad that spoke to where Bob was:

> *I find myself on the mountainside*
> *Where the rivers change direction*
> *Across the Great Divide*

He played *Silent Night* too. "Bob seemed content," Paul says. "He was there, in the moment; he was right there." The music did soothe him, Tony Gross remembers. "He was much more peaceful than the day before. He seemed to be looking up at the ceiling. His eyes were open, and I thought he was having a conversation. He was here, but he was somewhere else too."

Father Jim Schwartz gave Bob the last rites, as he had several times before when Bob's death appeared imminent. Patty, their friend Sandi York, and I prayed a few prayers.

Patty dozed off in the chair next to Bob. As always, the television was on, tuned to the Discovery Channel. I turned my attention to the program. I held Bob's hand, and a show came on about the guillotine. It was one of those investigative programs. "Is there pain after the beheading?" the narrator asked. "Some experts say it can last for fifteen seconds or so, while the head may still be conscious, until the oxygen supply drains away."

Better that, I thought to myself, than what Bob is going through.

I do not feel the same today, however. Suffering is not always bad. It is always painful, by definition, but it is not always bad. In some cases it may be necessary if we are to resolve the deepest conflicts in the human experience.

Those conflicts are almost always between letting go and holding on. Do we try to keep our teenagers close to us—and risk keeping them dependent and immature when they should be moving into adulthood? Do we let go? How soon? It is a balancing act, and in finding our balance there is often suffering—spiritual, intellectual, emotional. Even when we want to do what is right, we cannot always find the path. But this suffering—the product of struggle—is good for us.

But this suffering— the product of struggle—is good for us.

It teaches us, matures us, and plants in us the seeds of compassion for all those people with whom we might otherwise lose patience.

In Bob's case, the suffering was the bitter fruit of the mother of all conflicts—between clinging to the life and the people he loved and giving in to the equally powerful pull of God's embrace. It is clear to me now that Bob did not know which was the right choice until his last moments, when peace—finally—erased all his doubt.

At four o'clock that Sunday afternoon, November 15, 1998, I went home, not certain but expecting this really was the end. At 10:15, Patty called Eric and Jenny to tell them that the drugs had finally kicked in and Bob was out of pain. This is the end, she told Eric. The two of them hurried to St. Mary's.

"We got in the room and Mom was there with Dad—holding his hand. Dad was still breathing, but real softly," Eric remembers. "It looked as if he had tears in his eyes. They were sort of moist. Mom was right. He was finally out of all the pain he had been in over that final week. So Jen and Mom went on one side and I was on the other. I held his hand and so did Mom. We told him that we loved him and that it was OK if he wanted to go—that we would be fine. After a few minutes, Dad went. I will say that it was very peaceful."

It was done. Shortly after 11 P.M., Bob Schwartz made his Last Jump, the one he'd sung about: "Into the black; No turning back; No telling what you may find." In our own often clumsy ways, all of us who traveled those last miles with him had helped him make that jump. That's what the Communion of Saints does. There was no way he could say no to his last jump, but because of all the support he had, I believe in the depth of my soul that Bob was finally able to say yes.

Bob's funeral was five days later, on Friday, November 20. It was held at Holy Family, the inner city gothic church from which his mother and father had been buried. It was a damp and rainy morning, perfect for a dirge. But there was to be no such thing.

The church was mobbed. Close to 1,000 people squeezed into the nave and choir loft (designed for maybe 700). Generations of McQuaid students, some of them wearing hockey jerseys, sat elbow to elbow. Parents of students, friends—close and distant—and family members sardined themselves into the pews. Some of the nurses and doctors and hospice workers who'd been with Bob through the cancer made a point of coming.

"I go to two or three patients' funerals a year," says Barbie Edwards, one of Bob's oncology nurses. "Certain ones I feel I have to go to. His was one of them. It was amazing. It was joyous, not sad."

The Schwartz family accompanied the casket down the center aisle. The procession moved slowly through the crowds that had spilled out of the pews. Standees had to turn sideways to allow the pallbearers and casket to pass.

If ever a funeral was a celebration of life, this one was. The gospel was from St. John: "I have glorified you on earth and finished the work that you gave me to do, I have made your name known to the people you took from the world to give me. They were yours, and you gave them to me and they have kept your word."

In his eulogy, Father Jim reflected on those verses: "This is also how

I would describe my good friend Bob Schwartz.... Bob's prayer to his God is the same as the prayer of Jesus. Bob has finished the work the Lord has given him to do. Indeed he has made the Lord's name known."

Bob prepared his funeral—all of it—Father Jim said. And when he asked Bob what he should preach about, "Bob, the teacher, recalled a familiar question he always asked his students: *Who are you?*

"Who are you as we gather this morning to celebrate Bob's entrance into eternal life? We can't stay static. Life changes us. Life can pass us by unless we realize and claim who we are. We need to know who we are as God sees us, as the world sees us, and as others see us."

Bob's life was all about discovery, and his question invites us all to take stock of every day, to start fresh and look ahead. That was how he lived, and that is how he died.

The eulogy was the perfect segue to a poem written specifically for Bob by folksinger Tommy Makem and read at the funeral:

> *Sound the bright cord and sing the sweet song*
> *Let voices from the heart ring out*
> *Across space and time, and*
> *Fill the world with the sounds*
> *To strengthen the weary*
> *To comfort the downtrodden*
> *To free the oppressed;*
> *To lighten the load of the burdened*
> *And to brighten the weary heart*
>
> *Bob, your life was such a song*
> *Rejoice and know that you have touched*
> *And enriched those of us who were privileged*
> *To hear and bear witness*
> *To your joyous life song*
> *Let the song ring out.*

Bob Schwartz did not just sing songs, he became the songs. They shaped who he was and what he wished for others. Tommy Makem had it just right. Perhaps it takes a poet, I thought, to know one.

His funeral was shaped by his words. The images were his. The images were *him*. He could not let the occasion pass without an absurdly (apparently) inappropriate moment. As Joe Dady sang the satirical *Isn't it Grand?* there was an awkward silence. Should we laugh out loud? Recoil? Pretend to find some deep meaning in it? It was Bob's last joke:

> *Look at the coffin with the golden handles*
> *Isn't it grand boys to be bloody well dead?*

> *Chorus:*
> *Let's not have a sniffle, let's have a bloody good cry*
> *And always remember the longer you live, the sooner you'll bloody well die*

> *Look at the flowers, all bloody withered*
> *Isn't it grand boys to be bloody well dead?*

> *Look at the preacher, bloody nice fellow (bloody sanctimonious)*
> *Isn't it grand boys to be bloody well dead?*

> *Look at the mourners, bloody great hypocrites*
> *Isn't it grand boys to be bloody well dead?*

> *Look at the widow, bloody great female*
> *Isn't it grand boys to be bloody well dead?*

It takes a gutsy man to mock his own death and to risk offending the friends and family who've come to mourn him. It takes an insightful man to know his friends would take it as it was intended—an opportunity to laugh at their own vulnerability, at the rituals we use sometimes to hide our grief or at least to confine it. Once again, Bob used humor to short-circuit the mourning—his own and ours.

But Bob knew his friends well. And he knew that deep inside many of us would wrestle with our own guilt at wishing he would die so we could move on with our own lives. He was saying, "Don't worry, we're all going to die. And I beat you all."

As they carried him out of the church, his CD played. The sounds of *I Gave You Each Other* filled the church. They played it through twice. These were Bob's words, in his own voice:

> *I gave you each other*
> *Take care of each other*
> *You are all you've had*
> *In good times and in bad*
> *Be friends to each other*

> *What about the one whose heart is torn?*
> *Spends her nights sitting, wishing she had not been born*
> *She needs you to see through all her tears*
> *To tell her it gets better with the passing of the years*

> *What about the one who can't be healed?*
> *No amount of words can take the pain when that's revealed*
> *But kisses, prayers, cards and hugs just might*
> *Help him gather strength to fight this seeming hopeless fight*

> *What about the ones who are left behind?*
> *Thinking they can't handle life that's truly been unkind*
> *Well, I don't give you more than you can stand*
> *And if you hold together then you'll hold a million hands*

The last verse played again and again in my head. "I don't give you more than you can stand." It was Bob's last message: You'll be all right if you just hold on to each other. It was advice he lived by and died by. It was part of his creed—a community of believers keeping the faith and interceding with and for each other.

The funeral was a release. Bob had found rest, and now so did his family and friends.

Four days later, Bob's ashes were buried at Webster Union Cemetery, a small quiet graveyard off the beaten path. It was another cold and gray afternoon. The wind snapped against our faces, its sting bringing tears to eyes that would have been moist anyway

It was, ironically, Bob and Pat's twenty-fifth anniversary. There were maybe fifteen or twenty of us gathered. Patty, Eric and Jenny held red roses; the rest of us, carnations. After Father Jim committed Bob to God, we dropped our flowers into the small hole, on top of his urn.

I remember thinking how small Bob had become, at first wasted by the cancer and now reduced by fire to a small box of ash. It was a humbling moment—one to remember the admonition given at the start of every Lent as the smudge of ash is applied to our foreheads: "Remember, human, that you are dust, and unto dust you shall return."

And yet, as the body returns to nothingness, the spirit soars. Live a good life, and in death you become large. You become the bridge others will use to find their own way to God. That's a good life's work. It was Bob's life's work.

See How He Lives On

I t is but a foolish man who thinks in death he's gone; Look in love at what he did; you'll see how he lives on." That's what Bob Schwartz said in his song, *To Seek a Newer World*. The words apply to us all.

We are all tempted to want to leave a visible footprint as proof of our existence: a building with a plaque on it, a stained glass window in a church, a big check to a charity, or a book with our name on the spine.

But the best legacy is the product of choices made—decisions that make us better people and allow us to touch the lives of the people around us. Making good choices was what Bob was all about.

As Vicki Bida said, "Most people get cancer, and you send them a card. It's their business, and you leave them alone. Bob forced you to deal with it. He wasn't going to do it alone. I'm so glad I knew him."

He gave people friendship. He lived for his relationships. When he connected with students, they never forgot him. Bob didn't advocate inserting yourself into other people's affairs when they clearly want to you to butt out. But he rejected the idea that we can ignore each other, or walk away from their hard times using "It's none of my business" as an excuse.

When he got cancer, he applied the same principle to himself—only in reverse: He expected people to stay with him. He never demanded it. He just *expected* it.

If you fear life, you will be too afraid to fight for it when the time comes. If you see the world as hostile and out to get you, you will surrender quickly to death, convinced you never had a chance. If you are angry at the world, you will die angry with God.

If you are Bob Schwartz, however, you believe anything is possible. You believe you can change the world, so naturally you believe you can beat cancer. And you know, no matter what happens, you can count on your friends. You can count on them to help you, and you can count on them to be there as a reason for you to keep trying. Even when you figure out you can't stop the cancer, you believe every day you stay alive is a day you can matter for someone, somehow. So you fight on. Bob surrounded himself with people all his life. He did the same thing in death.

Attitude is more a product of behavior than it is the result of external circumstances.

Bob's attitude didn't just happen. He didn't have an optimism gene that gave him a leg up on the pessimists and the naysayers. Attitude is more a product of behavior than it is the result of external circumstances. Bob looked for the good in people; it became his habit. When he got cancer, he naturally looked for a bright side—he might beat it, or at least he could use it as an opportunity to reach out to others and to use the disease to teach another lesson or two.

"In the dying process, a lot of people close down," Father Jim Schwartz says. "Their lives become smaller, simpler. Their world becomes their home, and then their bedroom, and then just their bed. Bob was so people oriented that he would defy the pain. He would do anything to reach another person, to meet someone new."

I'm sure Bob had no idea how his battle would end; he just knew he had to fight it. He believed early that he'd be the exception. He wanted to show his students that they must believe in themselves and never give up. He experimented with strategies to convince himself that all was well—the coffee filters, the CD, the recycling, going to work, looking for projects. He wanted to see if that would keep him alive or at least buy him more time. And those of us in the audience of his farewell tour wanted to see too.

As he got sicker, he wanted the children and his students to see that they are the best judges of themselves, and that they should never surrender, never give up. It was what he always taught in the classroom, and now he had to measure up to what he said. He also had to measure up to the expectations he put to music.

On his fortieth birthday, Paul Swiatek was reading a meditation book when he came upon a passage that reminded him immediately of his teacher Bob Schwartz: "We must not accept the judgment of others as a measure of our own self worth. Instead, we should live our lives in simplicity…. Since we need not expend energy in putting on airs or maintaining a position, we are actually free to cultivate the best parts of our personalities."

All teachers love to know they have made such an impression that students hear their words and remember them in unforeseen places decades after they've left the classroom. Bob made people think about life, about their own lives, about what matters, about the spiritual treasures that are worth so much.

And yet he never seemed to pull back and take stock of his own spiritual life. "Usually, in the first part of life, people focus on the outer journey," says Father Jim. "Mattering means building a legacy in the world. Then, in the second half, 'mattering' takes on a new meaning. What matters is not the outer journey, but the inner journey. All the trappings of life become insignificant."

Bob never took that inner journey. "When I'd try to get him to talk about the dying process," Father Jim remembers, "he'd always say 'Let's talk later.' But later never came."

Bob's reluctance to talk directly about the crisis that was upon him always threw me. It didn't seem to square with the man for whom the intangibles were all that mattered. "He was very genuine," Father Jim says. "The interaction was all. But like his father, he did not have soul conversations. His family and his friends sustained him."

This lack of piety remains a mystery to me, but I have come to accept it—even if I cannot understand it. For Bob, good works were prayers. Reaching out was reaching in. There was no distinction. And it worked for him. He didn't prepare for death because he was too busy living. His real courage was apparent in the way he lived up to the words he wrote:

> *Whatever You wish for me*
> *I accept lovingly,*
> *I accept willingly*
> *I accept lovingly.*

Bob did not retreat from his friends when the dark night of the soul came over him. You could see his pain and his fear. He didn't talk about it, but it was there. You could see his body breaking down. He was afraid to die, but he was more afraid of not living. And that is where Bob's true dignity was so obvious.

I would never judge the soul of anyone who decides, when death is inevitable, to ask for the drugs that would end the pain for good. But there is another way, says Debbie Sigrist, the hospice nurse: "The body disintegrates. There is nothing we can do about that. You have to wait for the body to unravel. You have to move the locus of control from your body to your mind. As you disintegrate, where does dignity lie? The only dignity is in the spirit."

In death, dignity comes from a life lived well. Pain is never to be sought, but it is not always to be avoided. Bob did all he could to minimize the pain. He was not afraid of increasing his reliance on drugs. But he used the drugs to hold on, not to help him let go. Sometimes that meant taking himself off a drug or refusing a medical procedure as a way of retaining control and choice. And when it was time for him to go, he needed his friends. He needed to be part of something bigger than himself—the Communion of Saints, praying together as Jesus instructed us and picking up one another when we stumble on our way back to God.

I learned from Bob Schwartz there is no right way to die, only a right way to live. Each of us is responsible for the person we become. We construct that person from the choices we make over a lifetime. It is easy to tell ourselves that small things don't matter. We beg off a dinner engagement, telling a friend that we have a cold when we do not. We pretend we forgot a promise to help a neighbor move a sofa. These are small things, but when we lie to give ourselves an excuse for a broken promise, we make lying easier. When we keep our promises, or at least have the courage to ask to be let out of a commitment, we fortify our character. We become better people. We build the spiritual confidence we will need to complete our own last jump.

If we live well, we will die well. Death may not be easy, it may not make sense to ourselves or to others, but it will be all right. It will be what it is.

We will tire of the deathwatch; we will sometimes resent it. But dying people do not owe the people around them a quick departure. Dying people are entitled to the time they need, and the time God gives them. There is nothing selfish about taking it. And there is nothing selfish about involving the people around us—insofar as they are able and willing—in our deaths. It *is* their business, if they choose to make it so.

A year after Bob's death, I asked Tommy Makem to name a song that reminded him of the Bob he knew. He didn't hesitate. "Rabbie Burns' *A*

Man's a Man for a' That," he said.

The song by the eighteenth-century Scottish poet/songwriter Robert Burns expresses confidence in the ultimate victory of virtue over pretension, of honesty over wealth:

> *Is there for honest poverty*
> *That hings (hangs) his head, an a' that?*
> *The coward-slave we pass him by—*
> *We dare be poor for a' that*
> *For a' that an a' that,*
> *Our toils obscure, an a' that,*
> *The rank is but the guinea's stamp,*
> *The man's the gowd (gold) for a' that.*

> *What though on hamely (ordinary) fare we dine,*
> *Wear hoddin grey (coarse gray cloth), an' a' that?*
> *Gie (Give) fools their silks, and knaves their wine—*
> *A man's a man for a' that.*
> *For a' that, an' a' that,*
> *Their tinsel show, an' a' that,*
> *The honest man, tho e'er sae (though ever so) poor,*
> *Is king o' men for a' that.*

> *Ye see yon birkie ca'd (a sprightly fellow called) 'a lord,'*
> *Wha (Who) struts, an' stares, an' a' that?*
> *Tho' hundreds worship at his word,*
> *He's but a cuif (fool) for a' that.*
> *For a' that, an' a' that,*
> *His ribband (ribboned) star, an' a' that,*
> *The man o' independent mind,*
> *He looks an' laughs at a' that.*

A prince can mak (make) a belted knight,
A marquis, duke, an' a' that!
But an honest man's aboon (above) his might—
Guid (Good) faith, he mauna fa' (must not fault) that!
For a' that, an' a' that,
Their dignities, an' a' that,
The pith o' sense an' pride o' worth,
Are higher rank than a' that.

Then let us pray that come it may
(As come it will for a' that),
That Sense and Worth o'er a' the earth,
Shall bear the gree (come off best) an' a' that!
For a' that, an' a' that,
It's comin yet for a' that,
That man to man the world o'er
Shall brithers (brothers) be for a' that.

Why is poverty more honest than wealth? It is because honesty is the true measure of wealth. It matters not that we eat common food and wear simple clothes. The honest man, though ever so poor, is king, for all that.

People may dote on the rich and powerful, but the man of independent mind laughs at it all. He is above the pretense. Good sense shall carry the day. And those who rise above the foolish pursuit of fame and wealth shall live as brothers.

That was Bob Schwartz. Committed, finally, to what mattered most. He wrote it. He sang it. He taught it. He chose it. He lived it. He loved it. He died it.

One unusually warm January afternoon, I visited Rochester's Vietnam War Memorial to see for myself the bollard bearing the name of John B. Tette. His marker, like those of all the graduates of Aquinas Institute, had been decorated for Christmas with a red velour bow and a rose.

I found two passages cut in stone as memorials to the soldiers remembered there. Both apply also to Bob Schwartz, who likewise fought the good fight.

One passage is by Tim O'Brien from his novel *The Things They Carried*. In part it reads:

> They carried the soldier's greatest fear, the embarrassment of dishonor. They crawled into tunnels, walked past and advanced under fire, so as not to die of embarrassment. They were afraid to die, but too afraid to show it. They carried the emotional baggage of men and women who might die at any moment. They carried the weight of the world. They carried each other.

The second passage is etched into a slab of polished black granite, at the opposite end of the monument, past the 280 bollards commemorating all those from Rochester who died in Vietnam. The words are those of Major Michael Davis O'Donnell, a helicopter pilot who was killed in action on March 24, 1970:

> *Take what they have left,*
> *And what they have taught you*
> *With their dying,*
> *And keep it as your own.*

I sat and read those words slowly. Two times. Three times. Repeating them to make them my own. They have endured because they ring true. I suddenly realized that Bob Schwartz's story was not what it seems to be from a distance—the account of a man taken down by cancer. His story is really about the inner strength and happiness that comes from choosing to spend oneself for others. His story is proof that freedom ennobles us not when we exercise our right to make selfish choices but when we consciously choose to be part of a community much larger than ourselves. Together is how we will ultimately find God.

Bob Schwartz's story is everyone's story, and that is why I have told it.

Other titles in the *American Catholic Experience* series

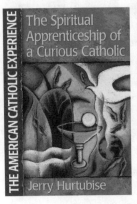
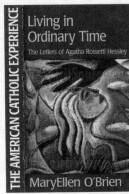
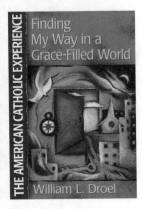

Available from booksellers or call (800) 397-2282
www.actapublications.com

The Musical Legacy of Bob Schwartz

To purchase a CD of Bob Schwartz's songs
e-mail robertschwartz1998@msn.com